Hazardous Waste

HAZARDOUS WASTE

Allen Stenstrup

Educational Consultant
Helen J. Challand, Ph.D.
Professor of Science Education, National-Louis University

Technical Consultant
Steven Lester
Director, Citizens Clearinghouse for Hazardous Waste

CHILDRENS PRESS®
CHICAGO

A production of B&B Publishing, Inc.

Project Editor: Jean Blashfield Black
Editor: Terri Willis
Designer: Elizabeth B. Graf
Cover Design: Margrit Fiddle

Artist: Valerie A. Valusek
Computer Makeup: Dori Bechtel
                    Dave Conant
Research Assistant: Marjorie Benson
Research Consultant: Colleen Shine

Printed on Evergreen Gloss
50% recycled preconsumer waste
Binder's board made from 100% recycled material

Library of Congress Cataloging-in-Publication Data

Stenstrup, Allen
    Hazardous waste / Allen Stenstrup
         p. cm. -- (Saving planet earth)
    Includes index.
    Summary: Explains what hazardous wastes are, how they are produced, and
why it is difficult to dispose of them.
    ISBN 0-516-05506-2
    1. Hazardous wastes — Juvenile literature. [1. Hazardous wastes.
2. Pollution.] I. Title. II. Series.
    TD1030.5.S74   1991
    363.72'87--dc20   91-25864
                                                              CIP
                                                              AC

Cover photo—© Imtek Imagineering/Masterfile

TABLE OF CONTENTS

Chapter One

Love Canal: The Beginning

IT WAS RECESS TIME at 99th Street School in Niagara Falls, New York. The students dashed from their classrooms to the playground. The sun was shining—the heavy rain of the previous night had stopped. Many children splashed through the puddles of rainwater scattered on the hard surface of the playground.

But these were not ordinary puddles. They were black, with a kind of rainbow look on the surface. There was a chemical smell in the air, and the children who played near the puddles soon felt their eyes watering. It certainly wasn't the best place to play, but it was the only playground the students had.

Within 24 hours, some of the children who ran through the puddles developed rashes. Parents and teachers soon realized that something was very wrong on the playground. In fact, it turned out that something was very wrong in a large part of Niagara Falls, something that made people realize that the whole country—perhaps the whole world— had a serious problem.

A long and complex series of events led up to the dangerous school-playground situation. It was destined to make Love Canal, that section of Niagara Falls, one of the best-known neighborhoods in the United States.

Model City Turned Poison

In the early 1890s, William T. Love designed a "model city" to be built near the famous Niagara Falls in northwestern New York. The abundant water would produce cheap electricity that industries could use for power. The natural beauty of the falls would attract people to the area.

Love's plan was to construct a deep canal about 6 miles (10 kilometers) long and divert water from the Niagara River into the canal. This flowing canal would be used to produce electricity for factories built along the shore. At that time electricity could not be sent over long distances, so businesses had to build close to a power source. Construction of the canal started in the mid-1890s.

The "model city" soon became a financial disaster. Before the project was completed, the process of making alternating electric current (AC) was invented. With AC current, electricity can travel long distances, so industries no longer had to be located next to their power source. The project went broke. The canal building was stopped. It left behind a huge trench that was 1 mile (1.6 kilometers) long, 10 to 40 feet (3 to 12 meters) deep, and 50 to 80 feet (15 to 24 meters) wide.

However, chemical companies were still attracted to the area because of the abundant water supply, and such companies grew rapidly. One of the first was the Hooker Electrochemical Company, which started in 1905 with 75 workers. It produced chlorine (a greenish, poisonous liquid) and a chemical called caustic soda. The company grew steadily and opened several new chemical plants in the area. In 1947, Hooker purchased the old canal site—a sale of that land that would affect families in this area for years to come.

Hooker used the old trench as a dump for its waste chemicals. The company buried more than 43 million pounds (19.5 million kilograms) of chemical wastes from nearby plants in the old canal-that-never-was. The chemical plants produced these wastes in the process of making pesticides and plastics. They included lindane, a highly toxic

pesticide; benzene, an industrial solvent known to cause the blood cancer called leukemia; and hundreds of pounds of dioxin, one of the most dangerous chemicals known.

By 1953 the canal was filled with metal barrels called drums—all of them full of these waste materials. The company closed the dump. They covered the site with a layer of clay soil and then added topsoil and grass. Few people in the area paid attention to either the dumping of the wastes or the closing of the dump.

More and more people were moving to the area, so the city of Niagara Falls decided to buy the Love Canal site and develop it. For a token payment of $1, the school board purchased the 16-acre (6.4-hectare) site. In the bill of sale, Hooker Electrochemical Company warned that the area contained buried chemicals and that the company was not responsible if anyone was injured by them.

An infrared photo of the Love Canal area shows that nothing grew over the hazardous-waste site. What shows as red in the photo is really green vegetation.

9

The school board ignored the warning and started to build a new elementary school in 1954. The construction company discovered several chemical pits on the first site chosen for the school, so the site was moved about 85 feet (25.9 meters). Part of the new playground was put directly over the old canal.

The 99th Street School opened in the fall of 1955. More than 400 children attended the school, playing at recess and after school over the old canal site. During the next several years many new homes were built with their backyards bordering on the old canal.

Over the next ten years some children developed rashes after playing around the schoolyard. A number of residents complained of chemical smells in their basements. Holes rusted in the buried drums and they collapsed, causing the ground to sink in some areas. Neighborhood dogs often had clumps of hair mysteriously fall out. But since the chemical industry was so well established in the area, people were not greatly concerned.

From 1965 to 1978, residents became used to odors and black oily liquids oozing into their basements. More soil sank, exposing more barrels and chemicals. For several years in the mid-1970s, a great increase in rain and snow caused flooding in the area. The barrels were now at least 20 years old and decaying rapidly. On the baseball diamond behind the school, the ground opened up near second base, and another pit appeared in the outfield. The principal of the school closed this part of the playground until these pits could be filled properly.

Complaints from local residents increased—and so did their health problems. Several children in the neighborhood were born with serious birth defects, such as two sets of teeth and heart problems. Four mentally retarded children were born to families that lived next to the old canal. The number of cases of cancer, epilepsy, liver and kidney problems, lung disease, and headaches was far above normal.

The public got angrier and finally, in 1978, the school was closed. Investigators found that the air, soil, and water around the canal were heavily polluted with a wide range of deadly chemicals.

Love Canal became the center of national and international attention. All the occupants of 236 homes were evacuated—men, women, and children. The state of New York purchased the homes from the residents. The area was fenced off and signs were erected warning people to keep out of the old canal site.

After more testing, an additional 780 families were evacuated from the area in 1980. President Jimmy Carter declared the site a Federal Disaster Area. This was the first time in history that a national emergency was declared as a result of pollution instead of tornadoes or floods.

More than 200 chemicals had been found in the wastes. The suffering the residents endured, the growing mistrust of government and industry, and the slow response of officials to the danger turned Love Canal into a true disaster.

Homes closest to the Love Canal waste site had to be demolished because they could never be safe places for people to live.

The impact that Love Canal had on the world was tremendous. Everywhere, people began to question the safety of waste dumps in their neighborhoods. In the following years, fourteen other sites near Niagara Falls were labeled as dangerous. At three of these locations, Hooker had dumped almost 350 million pounds (157.5 million kilograms) of chemicals, nearly ten times the amount buried at Love Canal.

Love Canal Today

The two streets and the houses on the canal are gone, bulldozed under a 40-acre (16-hectare) mountain of clay. The 99th Street School is demolished. Almost all of the chemical waste is still buried there, but now it is covered by layers of clay and plastic. A system of pipes was installed to collect chemicals from around the old canal, so they could be treated and disposed of more safely. A 3-foot (0.9-meter) layer of clay and a plastic liner were put on top to prevent rain from mixing with the chemicals. Another 18-inch (46- centimeter) layer of topsoil was added and seeded with grass.

The cost of the cleanup has been tremendous—more than $250 million for the 10-block area. It will cost an additional $31 million to clean the contaminated soil dredged from creeks and sewers in the area. More than $14 billion in lawsuits were filed against Hooker.

Would you like to buy one of the homes that was evacuated? In 1990 the government said that some parts of Love Canal are safe to live in again. More than 200 people expressed an interest in buying the boarded-up houses. And on November 28, 1990, the first family to re-occupy a home in the once-evacuated area moved in.

Why would people want to buy homes in the nation's

A sign used when transporting hazardous materials. It is one of several shown throughout this book.

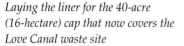

Laying the liner for the 40-acre (16-hectare) cap that now covers the Love Canal waste site

The cap that now covers the Love Canal waste site consists of three layers—plastic liner, clay, and topsoil. All of them are shown in the picture above.

first environmental disaster area? Some say it's the most studied area of the world and must be safe if the government says so. Others like the prices—they are 20 percent lower than other houses in Niagara Falls. And some potential buyers say there are environmental problems no matter where you live in the world.

In 1890, Love Canal was part of one person's dream. In 1980, it was causing nightmares for thousands of people. When Hooker Electrochemical Company (now part of Occidental Chemical Corporation) produced the waste material, the company was making products that people were anxious to buy. And Hooker disposed of the waste in a way that was acceptable at that time. Years later, a new generation suffered the results of that acceptance.

The events at Love Canal focused attention on similar hazardous-waste sites around the world. The Environmental Protection Agency (EPA)—the U.S. government agency responsible for protecting the environment—has more than 30,000 potentially dangerous hazardous-waste sites to investigate. Other countries have similar numbers. It will be the task of years to clean up old waste. In addition, we must develop new ways of manufacturing that do not produce hazardous wastes that poison our environment.

Chapter 2

Global Warning

LOVE CANAL MADE HEADLINES everywhere. The whole world was becoming aware of the way chemicals were disposed of and the dangers of those methods. However, Love Canal was not the first such problem, nor will it be the last. Hazardous-waste problems have begun to be recognized all over the globe.

Minimata, Japan

Minimata is a small, quiet fishing village in Japan. There, in 1953, several cases of what later became known as "Minimata disease" were discovered among fishermen and their families. Many victims went blind or had brain damage and other nervous-system disorders. Local doctors believed that the illnesses were caused by eating shellfish that naturally produced a harmful substance.

But the health problems continued. More than 40 people died in 1956, and many more became ill. Finally, doctors realized that the victims were suffering from mercury poisoning—and the source of the mercury was a favorite food of the villagers. Many of them ate fish and shellfish that had taken in a chemical called methylmercury. When digested by humans, methylmercury affects the brain. By 1983, more than 300 people had been killed by Minimata disease and more than 1,500 others showed symptoms.

Researchers discovered that a local plastics company, Chisso Chemical, had dumped more than 400 tons (360 metric

Though fish is the main food of many Japanese people, they hesitated to eat it after learning that nearby waters had been contaminated with mercury and other chemicals.

tons) of mercury into Minimata Bay. The mercury did not spread out in the ocean, but instead, it accumulated in the shellfish. It took years to recognize the problem and identify the source. It also caused great human suffering.

Bhopal, India

In a poor, densely populated area of Bhopal, India, on the night of December 2, 1984, most people were fast asleep. Many never woke up.

A large Union Carbide Corporation chemical plant that produced pesticides was operating near Bhopal. Shortly after midnight, more than 25 tons (22.5 metric tons) of methyl isocyanate (MIC) gas escaped from a storage tank there. MIC is a toxic chemical used to produce Sevin, a pesticide. Many people were killed as the MIC cloud spread into their homes. Others tried to get away from the fumes, choking and coughing as they ran.

The release of MIC was finally stopped two hours later. According to official reports, a total of 3,828 people died, more than 200,000 were injured, and six years later, 2,720 people still suffered from permanent disabilities, mostly associated with damage to lungs, eyes, and women's reproductive organs.

The release of MIC was caused when an unhappy employee attempted to spoil a batch of the chemical by adding water to it. The water caused a chemical reaction that resulted in a cloud of poison gas. Because the incident took place when most people were sleeping, thousands were caught in the deadly cloud that settled on the area in the night air. Even worse, civil authorities had no emergency evacuation plans to help the townspeople in an emergency.

The next morning, hundreds of doctors and nurses volunteered to help. The United States government and Union Carbide sent medicine and medical experts.

In 1989, Union Carbide agreed to pay $470 million in compensation, directed by India's Supreme Court as "full and final" payment of all claims arising from the tragedy. Many victims remain dissatisfied with this settlement.

Basel, Switzerland

In the late 1980s, a group of scientists studying the shores of Europe's Rhine River were shocked at the damage they saw. More than 400,000 fish were dead. Hundreds of thousands of eels, usually very resistant to pollution, lay along the shores. Insects didn't buzz anywhere. More than 60 miles (96.6 kilometers) of the Rhine, known throughout the world for its natural beauty, was a lifeless strip of water.

It wasn't hard to learn what caused the problems. On November 1, 1986, a huge fire had erupted at the Sandoz chemical factory near Basel. As firefighters battled the blaze, drums of chemicals exploded, releasing dangerous chemicals into the river. More than 65 tons (58.5 metric tons) of pesticides and chemical dyes entered the river that night. Among them were parathion, mercury, and disulfoton, a very toxic insecticide.

A man whose sight was affected by the pesticide leak at Bhopal, India, being led by two others to a safer area

The fire at a chemical plant near Basel, Switzerland, in 1986 was put out very quickly, but officials had not yet discovered the damage done to the Rhine River by pollution.

Investigators looking into the accident discovered that a neighboring company had experienced a major spill of a herbicide called atrazine the day before. They learned that other chemical factories frequently discharged more harmful chemicals into the Rhine than they were legally allowed to.

The people living in the area were greatly affected by the pollution. The water from the river could not be used for drinking for a long time. Even now, though local residents are again allowed to drink the water, the dangers of other health problems persist. The Rhine River today is one of the most polluted rivers in the world.

FACT

Lead paint is no longer used in the United States, but it remains on the walls of many homes, especially in poor urban areas. Small children often swallow chips of it. Eating these paint chips has caused severe learning disabilities in many children, because the lead causes brain damage.

Elizabeth, New Jersey

Picture the scene investigators found near the Elizabeth River in Elizabeth, New Jersey, in 1979. A colorful variety of metal drums covered a warehouse yard that was bigger than three football fields. In some places the barrels were stacked four or five high. More than 40,000 drums containing toxic chemicals, acids, solvents, and other industrial wastes were stored at this site.

Many drums were unlabeled and pockmarked with holes that oozed their unknown contents. The chemical seepage stained the barrels, corroding the steel. The puddles in the yard were spotted with oily rainbows, and the heavy smell of chemicals hung in the air.

A waste-disposal company owned the facility. Pesticides and flammable liquids were just some of the hazardous

Toxic fumes from a 1980 chemical warehouse fire in Elizabeth, New Jersey, forced schools to close in the city as well as across the river in Staten Island, New York.

chemicals the company had accumulated. Inside the warehouse, investigators found even more—liquids labeled "Nitro," several hundred pounds of explosive picric acid, and many cylinders of a toxic nerve gas. These chemicals can cause a wide range of human health problems, including breathing disorders, cancer, and birth defects.

The facility was in "imminent risk of fire and explosion," state officials declared. Cleanup procedures were developed and action started at once.

The cleanup wasn't complete, though, on April 21, 1980, when the site erupted into flames. Explosions rocked the region. Flames shot hundreds of feet into the air. Clouds of toxic smoke spread over parts of the city. The firefighters kept a close eye on several large gasoline storage tanks and propane gas tanks nearby. If the fire had reached these tanks, they might have exploded and thousands of people could have been injured. But the fire never spread that far.

Fortunately, about 10,000 barrels of the most dangerous materials had already been removed from the warehouse facility. Nevertheless, 30 firefighters were injured, and many local residents sought medical attention.

After the fire, the remaining drums were transported to a landfill site in northern New York, one that isn't very far from Love Canal.

FACT Near a plant where nuclear weapons were made in South Carolina, the radiation level of the drinking water source was found to be more than 400 times greater than the level considered safe by the U. S. Environmental Protection Agency.

Times Beach, Missouri

The cars and trucks that traveled the dirt roads of Times Beach used to raise plenty of dust. Townspeople complained about the mess it made in their homes and on their cars. The local government responded in the 1970s by hiring a private contractor to spray the road with an oil-based liquid that was supposed to hold the dust down. It worked. Today, there is no more dust. In fact, there is no more Times Beach.

The homes and stores and buildings that used to be Times Beach are now surrounded by a chainlink fence. Bold signs warn "HAZARDOUS AREA—DIOXIN—KEEP OUT." The town of 2,200 people was evacuated in 1983, and more than 400 sagging buildings are now boarded up. Weeds grow on lawns where children once played. Today Times Beach's only visitors are scavengers and looters.

The problems in Times Beach started when oil was sprayed over the roads to control dust. The oil used was con-

Times Beach, once a friendly community in Missouri, is now a "toxic ghost town." Even the exit sign for Times Beach has been removed from the nearest highway.

taminated with chemicals, including dioxin, benzene, and toluene. In 1983, when the Meramec River flooded the area's roadways, the chemicals spread throughout Times Beach.

The town was already under investigation because it was one of about 45 sites that received the contaminated oil. After the flooding, government officials found levels of dioxin 100 times higher than was considered safe for long-term contact. The only safe solution was for the government to buy the entire 1-square-mile (2.6-square-kilometer) area and close the town. The cost was more than $33 million.

Now, nearly a decade after the dioxin was discovered, Times Beach is being buried. More than 135,000 tons (121,500 metric tons) of soil contaminated with dioxin will be burned in an incinerator. The ashes, along with debris from the town, will be buried in a landfill and covered. Plans call for the area that was once Times Beach to be planted with trees and grass and turned into a riverway park. The community itself is just a memory.

Chernobyl, U.S.S.R.

On the morning of April 28, 1986, an alarm at the Forsmark Nuclear Power Plant in Sweden began to sound when a monitor found a high level of radiation in the air. Fearing a leak at the plant, officials evacuated most employees, while others searched frantically for the source of the leak.

Radiation consists of fast particles or waves of energy, such as those that come from the sun. But this kind of radiation—called radioactivity—is dangerous to living things.

Local residents were warned of the danger and hundreds of nearby schoolchildren were given iodine tablets to reduce

A giant radiation-proof casing was built over the nuclear reactor that exploded at Chernobyl in the Soviet Union. It will probably have to stay there for hundreds, even thousands, of years to prevent the radioactivity from doing more harm.

the effects of radioactive poisoning. But no leaks were ever found at the Forsmark plant.

High levels of radiation were soon detected in other areas of Sweden, and in Norway and Denmark, too. Swedish scientists began to look elsewhere for the source. Checking the wind patterns, they were able to trace the radiation to the city of Chernobyl in the Soviet Union.

For hours, Soviet officials maintained silence about the problem. Finally, at 9 P.M., a Soviet television announcement stated, "An accident has taken place at the Chernobyl power station, and one of the reactors was damaged."

The explosion at Chernobyl that released the deadly

radiation had occurred two days earlier. At about 1 A.M. on April 26, a test being performed on the reactor went wrong. Several of the safety devices on the reactor had been turned off, allowing a chain reaction (a continuous chain of atoms splitting apart) to take place. The chain reaction led to a tremendous explosion and the roof of the reactor was completely blown off. Enormous amounts of highly radioactive materials were released. Firefighters tried to put out a blaze that reached temperatures of more than 5000 degrees F. (2760 degrees C), but it was impossible. The fire burned out of control for several days. Finally, after helicopters dropped more than 5,000 tons (4,500 metric tons) of lead, sand, and boron on the reactor, the fire was put out.

By that time, the explosion and the fire had released radioactive particles high into the air. Winds carried them all over Europe. Crops were destroyed in Germany. In Britain, the sale of sheep that grazed on contaminated grass was banned. Many other governments banned the sale of milk.

In Chernobyl, local residents were evacuated about 36 hours after the explosion. More than 1,000 buses carried about 84,000 people from the area. Schoolchildren were evacuated all the way to Kiev, about 60 miles (96.6 kilometers) from Chernobyl.

The type of nuclear accident that so many people had long feared would happen had finally happened, and its effects were made worse by the slow response of the Soviet government.

The officially published death toll is 32, but thousands more were treated for radiation poisoning.

The reactor is now encased in concrete, but the region still suffers from the nuclear disaster. The government continues to monitor more than 576,000 people who were exposed to radiation during the accident. The soil in the area is lifeless, and many children are experiencing health problems. The cost of the cleanup has reached over $400 billion.

The accident was caused by a combination of human error and poor design. Who knows how many more people will die as a result of the accident? It may be hundreds of years before the full story of Chernobyl can be written.

Your Community — Your Environment

An Earth Experience

Disposal of hazardous wastes can have a great effect on your health and that of your neighbors. You can investigate the possibility of hazards in your community and help keep your community a safe place to live. Ask your parents or teacher or call your local city hall for the following information.

1. *Where does the water you drink at home come from? Where does the water you drink at school come from?*

2. *Where does the wastewater from your home go? Where does the wastewater from your school go?*

3. *Who is responsible for picking up your garbage? What is done with it?*

4. *Look around your neighborhood and school to see if there are any signs of pollution that might affect your water. Areas to look for include junkyards, landfills, storage tanks, industries, farmyards, field crops, and lawns or golf courses where people spread excessive fertilizers and pesticides. Can you locate any rivers or streams where rainwater from these places might run off? Do those rivers flow into your town's water sources?*

The Great Lakes

The Great Lakes are crucial to life in North America. They provide drinking water for more than 27 million Americans and 8 million Canadians. Home for millions of animals, birds, and fish, the Great Lakes are also vital for recreation and industry. Unfortunately, they've also been used as a dumping area for hazardous wastes for years.

The Great Lakes are among the largest freshwater lakes in the world—they hold 20 percent of the Earth's surface freshwater. But pollution and development have taken their toll on these magnificent lakes. In many places today the water is a threat to human health—swimming is prohibited and the fish are dangerous to eat.

In 1985, researchers identified 42 heavily polluted sites in the Great Lakes, called Areas of Concern, that require cleanup. Recently, the harbor at Erie, Pennsylvania, was added to the list. All but one of these Areas of Concern contain heavily polluted sediments, and many of these areas are seriously contaminated with hazardous wastes. See pages 72 and 73 for a map of the 43 Areas of Concern.

The harbor area at Waukegan, Illinois, is one of the most polluted. More than 1 million pounds (450,000 kilograms) of polychlorinated biphenyls (PCBs) were discharged by the local Outboard

This ditch leading into the harbor at Waukegan, Illinois, is the most polluted place in a badly polluted Area of Concern in Lake Michigan.

Marine Corporation. PCBs—oily, synthetic hydrocarbon compounds used mostly to insulate electrical equipment—are extremely toxic. The Outboard Marine Corporation has agreed to provide $21 million to clean up the area.

In Canada, Hamilton Harbour remains the most contaminated area. Along the shores of Lake Ontario, it is the site of a large steel industry that has released a variety of chemicals, including heavy metals, into the water. Raw sewage is another major source of pollution in the area.

Remedial Action Plans (RAPs) to deal with the problems have been agreed upon by the eight states that border the Great Lakes, and the Province of Ontario. The plans aim to clean up the Areas of Concern and restore such activities as swimming and fishing.

In many areas, the RAP recommendations have already begun to be followed, with the completion of new waste-treatment facilities or the removal of sediments. The plans will take years to complete. The efforts will improve the lakes' water quality, but the Great Lakes will probably never be totally cleaned.

These situations are some examples of the destruction being caused worldwide by hazardous wastes. The human health effects can be devastating, and the damage to the environment is just as bad.

The proper management and handling of hazardous wastes—one of the most important environmental issues now facing the world—is everyone's problem. As you will see later, the products we use in our homes often generate hazardous wastes, too. We all need to work together to protect our environment from the improper use, handling, and disposal of hazardous chemicals.

Chapter 3

Health at Risk

WARNING
NO FISHING

TOXIC
POLLUTION

FOR MORE INFORMATION ABOUT
CAMPAIGN FOR A CLEAN MISSISSIPPI RIVER,
CONTACT:

GREENPEACE

(202) 462-1177

WASHINGTON – 1436 U St. NW   Washington, DC 20009

A HAZARDOUS SUBSTANCE is a chemical that presents an unreasonable risk of injury to people or the environment when it is produced, transported, or disposed of. Such substances can be solid, liquid, or gas. They often have complex structures and tongue-twisting names like trichloroethylene (TCE) and polychorinated biphenyls (PCBs). Abbreviations are generally used to make them easier to read, write, and remember.

Chemicals—They're Everywhere

Everything we can see, feel, smell, or touch is made of chemicals—dirt, air, dogs, cake, flowers, bicycles—everything. The world is made of atoms, which are the building blocks of chemicals. Something made with only one kind of atom is an *element*. Examples include oxygen, mercury, and lead. Two atoms joined together make up molecules. Substances made with molecules are *compounds*, such as salt or dioxin. Salt is a very simple compound with just two atoms making up the molecule (NaCl, sodium chloride). Dioxin is extremely complex, containing hundreds of different atoms. Each combination of atoms in a molecule makes the chemical act in a different way. For example, hydrocarbons—chemicals made up of hydrogen and carbon—are present in petroleum. But there are many kinds of hydrocarbons, all with different arrangements of atoms.

Accidents, such as this one on a railroad, can release hazardous materials into the air, the water, and the soil.

Studying Molecular Structure

Chemicals come in many varieties. Some occur naturally in the Earth or in our atmosphere, while others are synthetic (man-made). Natural chemicals have always been on Earth, and people, plants, and animals have adapted to them in the amounts that exist naturally. Synthetic chemicals, however, are a very different story.

A natural chemical was first reproduced in 1828. A chemist duplicated it in the laboratory, and chemists were soon creating chemicals never before found on the Earth. The number of synthetic chemicals produced skyrocketed after World War II. Studies of sediments (accumulations of material that settle out of water, such as at the bottom of a lake) in the environment show that concentrations of many hazardous chemicals began rising rapidly about 50 years ago.

Worldwide, the chemical industry has created numerous synthetic compounds that affect our daily lives. Fuels, medicines, plastics, fibers, pesticides, solvents, and food additives

are just a few of the products involved. Many have made our lives longer and more pleasant, but some have also caused unforeseen problems.

Plastics processing involves numerous hazardous substances.

It is estimated that 70,000 chemicals are already being used on a regular basis by manufacturers around the globe. This year alone, between 500 and 1,000 new chemicals will be introduced. No one can anticipate all the effects of these chemicals.

FACT

When harmful substances can no longer be used, they become hazardous wastes. In the United States and Canada, government regulates the use and disposal of hazardous wastes. This is due to the drastically increased use of synthetic chemicals and their past history of improper disposal.

The U.S. Environmental Protection Agency (EPA) has defined hazardous waste as waste material that may pose a threat or hazard to human health or the environment when

"CREATE HAZARDOUS WASTE? WHO, ME?"

Photographs
Photofinishing produces silver, which can be toxic to aquatic life and micro-organisms

Paint
Paint sludges contain toxic heavy metals that could interfere with the operation of a sewage-treatment plant

Radios
Metal parts are plated with chromium and nickel for corrosion-resistance and appearance. These metals can be environmentally hazardous and toxic to humans

Clothing
Dyes are used to color fabric. Waste streams from the dyeing process may contain hazardous substances

Shoes
Tanning transforms hide into leather. A common pollutant from the tanning process is chromium, which is toxic to humans at very low dosages

Telephones
Chemical additives and raw materials are used in the production of plastic. They may be environmentally hazardous and toxic to humans if they enter the waste stream

Printed labels
During the printing process, waste inks are generated. The wastes are hazardous because they contain solvents and oils, which can be toxic to aquatic life and microorganisms

Paper products
Chlorine used to bleach paper creates toxic wastes that resist degradation. Trace amounts of dioxins may be generated in the process

not handled properly. These waste materials are often *by-products,* materials left after goods are produced. The manufacture of many things we like produces hazardous wastes—things like blue jeans, basketballs, computers, minibikes, and cosmetics. Plastic products themselves are safe to use, but many by-products are also produced when they are manufactured. Of the six main categories of chemicals that generate hazardous wastes, chemicals from five are used in making plastics.

Six Categories of Hazardous Wastes

The EPA has separated hazardous wastes into six categories. Chemicals that have the characteristics of several categories are listed in the group that best describes them.

Corrosive wastes have hearty appetites. They are strong enough to eat away steel drums or burn human skin. They are of special concern when being transported and stored, because they can corrode (eat away) containers and leak out. Examples of corrosive chemicals include strong cleaning materials and strong acids, such as those in car batteries.

Ignitable materials from the Vietnam War were packed in plastic and then vacuum -packed in small drums, which were stored in sand— and they still exploded of their own accord.

Ignitable wastes present a fire hazard because they may erupt into flames at a relatively low temperature. This causes not only the immediate danger of fire and smoke but also the risk of explosion and the threat that toxic gases may spread over an area. Paint remover, oils, and such chemicals as benzene are some examples.

Reactive wastes can explode or give off deadly fumes during handling and storage by mixing with water or by reacting to heat or pressure. These wastes include old weapons and ammunition, as well as some chemicals.

An Earth Experience

Chain Reactions

Nuclear power plants cause controversy. Likewise, the production of nuclear weapons disturbs lots of people. Both of these use radioactive material and deal with fission—the splitting of atoms.

Let's role-play the chain of events that occurs in fission. You will need a number of friends or classmates for this activity.

To make a bomb, one person stands in the middle and represents a free neutron, a bundle of neutral energy that is usually bound up in the nucleus of an atom. The neutron starts the reaction by squeezing the hands of the two people on either side. Follow the illustration to position your friends—the atoms—in all directions. In some cases, three or four hands are in contact. As soon as each person feels the squeeze of a hand, he or she passes it on to the next person. Notice that the amount of fission starts out small but moves rapidly in all directions. This movement represents the uncontrolled

Key.

— Arms

● Hands holding

⬤ Players

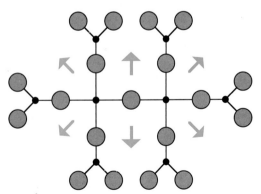

Radioactive wastes include materials with both high and low radioactivity. They can cause dangerous effects for thousands of years. Most radioactive wastes are produced at nuclear power plants and by research facilities.

Toxic wastes consist of chemicals that are poisonous. People exposed to these types of materials can develop health problems. Birth defects and cancer, illness, or such problems as nervousness and headaches could be related to toxic waste. Sometimes, even death can result from exposure to toxic waste. Lead, arsenic, mercury, and other chemicals

chain reaction that occurs in a bomb.

Fission in a nuclear power plant is controlled and lasts longer. Again, follow the illustration to arrange the players, who will act the role of atoms being struck by neutrons and splitting. Try to have the same number of "atoms" in each activity. In the first illustration, there are 18 atoms plus the free neutron.

Do some library research to find answers to the following questions:

1. What nuclear fuel is used in power plants?
2. What are fuel rods, the moderator, and control rods?
3. How does a reactor actually produce electricity?
4. What kinds of accidents can occur at these plants?
5. What are alpha particles, beta particles, and gamma emissions?
6. How are radioactive wastes from nuclear power plants disposed of? These include used reactor fuel, radioactive tailings, and any material exposed to radiation.

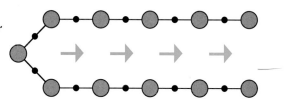

Peeling lead-based paint is often eaten by children living in older homes in poorer neighborhoods. Lead is a very toxic substance that causes numerous health problems.

including pesticides can be very dangerous.

The terms "hazardous wastes" and "toxic wastes" are often used to describe the same materials. But there is a difference. "Hazardous" is a term that refers to all wastes that pose a present or long-term threat to human health or the environment. The term "toxic" refers to a smaller group of substances that are poisonous and can cause death or serious injury to people or animals.

Infectious wastes are also toxic wastes, but they are a separate category. They consist of materials infected with some type of germ, bacteria, or virus that could cause disease in humans or animals. Infectious wastes often come from hospitals and medical and dental clinics. They may include things such as used hypodermic needles and human and animal tissue.

In order to protect human health, scientists must determine how corrosive, ignitable, reactive, and toxic each chemical is.

Human Health

Everyone is exposed to materials that can cause harm. Even common salt can be dangerous in large quantities—50 percent of adults weighing 180 pounds (81 kilograms) would die if they ate $1/2$-pound (0.2 kilogram) of salt quickly. Other chemicals can kill in much smaller amounts. For example, it would take only *one drop* of parathion, a pesticide, to kill an adult—even less to kill a child.

In some cases, hazardous substances don't kill people or animals, but they do cause burns or dizziness. In other cases, illnesses or disease may arise many years after people come in contact with hazardous substances. Exposure to hazardous substances may also do damage to the cell chromosomes, leading to birth defects in future generations.

It is extremely difficult for scientists to establish a link between human health and exposure to hazardous wastes. One of the biggest problems they face is the lack of information on the toxicity of thousands of chemicals that exist. According to the National Academy of Sciences, fewer than 10 percent of the agricultural chemicals and 5 percent of the food additives used in the United States have been fully tested. No one really knows what their long-term health effects might be.

Homes were built in Womelsdorf, Pennsylvania, on the site of an old factory that made lead arsenate pesticides. Eventually, the hazardous wastes began to ooze into people's basements, making them sick.

37

Pesticides sprayed onto fruit and other crops can work their way into the environment, eventually causing health problems from water supplies.

Exposure Time

An *acute exposure* is a single exposure to a hazardous material for a brief length of time. The time period could be as brief as a few seconds or as long as a week. One example of an acute exposure is the disaster in Bhopal, India. The acute effects of the exposure resulted in many deaths and illnesses. Acute effects are symptoms that appear immediately after exposure.

Workers removing old asbestos from ceilings must be protected from the dust, which can be harmful to lungs.

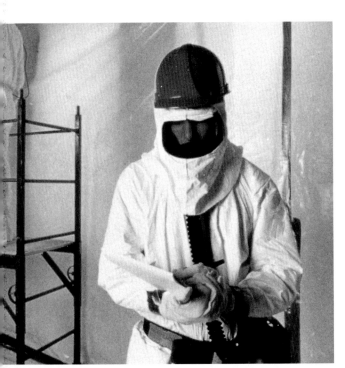

A *chronic exposure* occurs over a much longer period of time, usually with repeated exposures to a hazardous substance in low-level amounts. Chronic exposure often occurs in the workplace or in the home. The best-known example of chronic exposure is Love Canal, where residents lived next to the leaking hazardous-waste dump for years before the health effects were noticed.

Chronic health effects are delayed responses to hazardous substances—for example, cancer occurring following exposure to asbestos. A high percentage of people who are exposed for a long time to asbestos fibers die of lung cancer, but the disease may not appear for more than twenty years after the exposure.

Testing Procedures

Scientists who study the effects of chemicals are called toxicologists. They study affected people, and do laboratory studies with living things to determine the effects of chemicals.

The study of the distribution of various illnesses is called epidemiology. In this type of study, a researcher compares two separate groups of people.

For example, suppose a researcher wanted to determine the effects of Pesticide X. She would compare a group of people that had been exposed to the pesticide with a similar group of people in another area that had *not* been exposed to Pesticide X. If the

exposed group had a greater level of health problems, the researcher could say that Pesticide X was a potential danger to human health. But it's nearly impossible to prove that statement because of other factors that must be considered. Was the quality of the air in both areas the same? Were the

Technicians may use a mobile laboratory to go to hazardous-waste sites and determine the toxicity of the material being discarded.

Left, A flounder from the Baltic Sea, found to have cancerous tumors on its skin caused by infections related to pollution in the sea. Right, One of many cormorants that have hatched with crossed bills, believed to be an effect of toxic contamination of the food chain in the Great Lakes.

people's diets or exercise levels similar? Probably not. Therefore, Pesticide X can be considered a potential danger, but no positive conclusions can be drawn from this type of epidemiological study alone.

One way to confirm the results of an epidemiological study is to use laboratory studies. Small animals are given high doses of the chemical over a short period of time to see if they develop health problems. If they do, exposure to the chemical is considered a potential health risk for humans.

Both of these research methods have weaknesses. Establishing a link between hazardous substances and medical problems is extremely difficult. With chronic effects, health problems may take ten to twenty years to appear. However, toxicologists can make educated guesses on the risks of certain chemicals. The information they have been able to obtain definitely gives us reason to be concerned. The list of substances known or suspected to cause human health problems is growing.

Health Effects

Exposure to a hazardous substance might cause pain or itching. But it could also lead to very serious heart, lung, or kidney disease, or even death. Chemicals can affect cells in the body, and the effects can be great. Cancer and birth defects are among the most dangerous effects of exposure to hazardous chemicals.

Cancer is a disease in which certain cells suddenly start to grow uncontrollably and increase in number at a great rate. Soon they interfere with the normal functioning of one or more organs in the body.

There are more than one hundred forms of cancer, including lung, intestinal, and skin cancer. Chemicals that can cause cancer are called carcinogens. As scientists continue to research the effects of chemicals, more and more are found to be carcinogenic. About 7 to 10 percent of children born in the United States have birth defects, ranging from mild to very serious. Some causes of birth defects are drugs, radiation, and various chemicals. Another cause is mutations. Mutations are changes in the chromosomes (genetic material) supplied by the parents. Some hazardous materials appear to cause mutations, but more research is needed.

Sadly, the health effects of hazardous chemicals can rarely be reversed. Even after the hazardous chemical is removed, the health effects it caused can go on for years and even affect future generations.

Contact with Chemicals

People can come into contact with hazardous chemicals in a variety of ways, including breathing polluted air or drinking polluted water.

Airborne Substances. About 400 hazardous air pollutants can be found in the atmosphere, according to EPA investigators. In 1985, a study found that the amount of hazardous chemicals released into the air was about 80 million pounds (36 million kilograms) per year. But two years later, a new

study found that this figure greatly underestimated the problem. Actually, more than 2.4 *billion* pounds (1.1 billion kilograms) are released each year.

Hazardous airborne pollutants come from a variety of sources, such as industry smokestacks and auto exhaust. Most are created in the process of burning. The chemicals given off into the air as tiny particles or vapors include mercury, lead, and arsenic. These elements can cause cancer, damage to the nervous system, or kidney damage.

Toxic fibers are another type of airborne pollutant. Asbestos is the most common toxic fiber. It is used in more than 3,000 industrial processes because it is strong and resistant to heat. Workers use caution when handling asbestos, because it is known to be a potential cause of lung cancer when inhaled. For this reason, asbestos ceilings in many schools and other public buildings are now being removed or sealed.

Airborne pollutants can travel long distances in wind currents. About 25 percent of all the toxic substances that enter the Great Lakes come from air sources—some nearby and some far away. One chemical called toxaphene is used primarily in the southern states. Yet it has been found in island areas of Lake Superior, more than 1,000 miles (1,610 kilometers) away.

The health effects of airborne pollutants can be widespread. An area near New Orleans, Louisiana, has many chemical manufacturers that pour 400 million pounds (180 million kilograms) of toxics into the air each year. The rate of birth defects and lung cancer in this region is very high.

Groundwater. More than 100 million people in North America drink water from wells. The water, called groundwater, is pumped up from aquifers—underground formations that store and move water.

Groundwater near a leaky landfill being checked for its quality

Thousands of chemicals have been found in groundwater, and some of these chemicals may be harmful to people. Since many chemicals are odorless and tasteless, they go unnoticed. Medical experts are concerned about even very tiny amounts of chemicals mixing together in groundwater and becoming even more dangerous.

Testing for groundwater pollution is very expensive. It requires the drilling of many wells to follow the flow of the groundwater in order to take samples.

Surface waters may be put off limits to swimmers because they are polluted with hazardous materials. This beach is in Gdansk, Poland.

The state of Florida is almost completely surrounded by saltwater, so groundwater is an abundant, important resource there. It supplies most of the state's drinking water needs, and most other water needs as well.

Unfortunately, the region has many sources of groundwater contamination, such as pesticides and fertilizers, landfills, and areas where ocean water can invade fresh water. In addition, the soil cover over many of the aquifers is thin, making it easy for contaminants to seep in.

In response to these problems, Florida has a very effective groundwater protection program. The state monitors the groundwater closely. Industries that could possibly pollute the groundwater aren't allowed to locate near a water source. The state also does a lot to educate its residents and private industry about the need to protect the groundwater, telling them how to properly dispose of any harmful chemicals they use. These efforts are working to make sure that the people of Florida have safe water to drink and use.

Measuring Tiny Amounts

Scientists use a special measuring system to determine the level of chemicals in a sample. Many times the numbers they use will be in parts per million (ppm), parts per billion

Parts Per Million (ppm)	Parts Per Billion (ppb)	Parts Per Trillion (ppt)
1 second in 11.5 days	1 second in 32 years	1 second in 32,000 years
1 inch (2.5 centimeters) in 16 miles (25.8 kilometers)	1 step of a trip to the moon and back	1 grain of sugar in an Olympic-sized pool

(ppb), or even parts per trillion (ppt). These numbers indicate the levels of concentration. The amount of the measured substance is compared to a larger amount of the material it is in. The amounts may seem small, but the chemicals are often so toxic that just a little bit can do a lot of harm—or help. The active ingredient in aspirin is only 10 ppm.

The examples on the previous page will help you visualize these measurements. The chart on the next page will show you the health limits in parts per million or parts per billion of certain chemicals that are dangerous to us.

Discovering How Small a PPM Is

An Earth Experience

You can discover for yourself what 1 ppm means by doing one of the following activities.

1. Fill a measuring cup with water (that's about 1,000 drops). Add 1 drop of food coloring to the water with an eyedropper. Now take 1 drop of solution and add it to another cup of water, making 1 drop of food coloring per million parts of water (1 ppm). Can you see the coloring in the first cup? What about the second?

2. Count the number of unpopped kernels of popcorn in 1/4 cup. Take one kernel and wrap it with a small piece of masking tape or color it with a marker pen. Return it to your sample. Mix the popcorn. Try to find the marked kernel in your sample.

Add enough popcorn to your sample to make about 1,000 kernels. Your marked kernel is now 1 part per 1,000. To change to parts per million, you could add 1,000 more cups of popcorn, but you probably won't want to do that. Your marked kernel would be 1 part per million if mixed with the additional popcorn. Do you think you could find the marked kernel?

SOME IMPORTANT HAZARDOUS SUBSTANCES

Chemical	Source of Exposure	Method of Exposure	Limit of Exposure*	Health Effects
Benzene	solvents, pharmaceuticals detergent production	drinking water, air, on the job	.005 ppm	headaches, nausea, loss of muscle coordination, leukemia, bone-marrow damage
Dioxin	herbicides, waste incineration	pesticides, air, drinking water	**	cancer, birth defects, skin disease
PCBs	electronics, hydraulic fluid, fluorescent lights (banned since 1977)	eating fish, air	**	skin damage, possible gastro-intestinal damage, possibly cancer-causing
Mercury	fluorescent lamps, weather equipment, agricultural chemicals	eating fish, drinking water	.002 ppm	kidney damage, nausea, damage to brain and nervous system
Lead	paint, gasoline	air, drinking water, using paint and batteries	.02 ppm	headaches, irritability, mental impairment, brain, liver, and kidney damage
Cadmium	zinc processing, batteries, fertilizer processing	air, using fertilizers, on the job	.01 ppm	cancer in animals, damage to liver and kidneys

*Refers to the EPA Safe Drinking Water Limit
**No amount of these chemicals is considered safe.

Wildlife and Toxics

Great blue herons with crossed beaks, terns with club feet, fish with tumors—these are just a few of the ways that toxic wastes affect wildlife. Birds, especially, signal a warning to humans because toxics in their water concentrate in their fat cells. Other bird deformities caused by toxic wastes include missing eyes, small wings, and open stomachs.

Birds have historically acted as indicators of environmental problems, just as they do today. Bald eagles were almost wiped out by the pesticide DDT in the 1950s and 1960s. The toxic material made their egg shells too thin to develop.

The buildup of toxic chemicals in wildlife is related to the concept of a food chain. In a food chain, the toxic chemical

goes through *bioaccumulation*. Substances become more concentrated as they go up the food chain.

Let's consider the food-chain path of a harmful chemical like PCBs. Water may have 0.000003 ppm of PCBs in it. The PCBs are carried by microscopic water plants, called phytoplankton, and then microscopic water animals, called zooplankton, eat these plants. Minnows then eat the zooplankton. The minnows now have 0.5 ppm of PCBs. A coho salmon eats several minnows, acquiring 2 ppm of PCBs. A bird of prey eats lots of coho salmon and has 25 ppm. Humans become part of this food chain if they eat the fish. That's why many states warn women and young children to either stop eating fish or cut down considerably.

Mammals can also be affected by PCBs. For example, studies have shown that PCBs greatly reduce the reproduction rate of minks.

Other wastes can harm wildlife as well. The Gulf of the Farallones National Marine Sanctuary near San Francisco, California, is threatened by a large radioactive-waste dump. At least 47,500 barrels with plutonium and other wastes were dumped in the sanctuary between 1946 to 1975. Now, most of the barrels are corroded and leaking, and many have burst from the water pressure. Scientists have begun studying the harmful effects this waste has on marine life.

Nature is giving us the warning signs that hazardous substances are entering the environment. Unfortunately nature is also the innocent victim of the hazardous chemical world that humans have created.

Ink wastes from a factory in Altoona, Pennsylvania, were illegally dumped. The workers cleaning up the site must wear protective clothing and breathe through respirators until the toxicity of the waste has been determined.

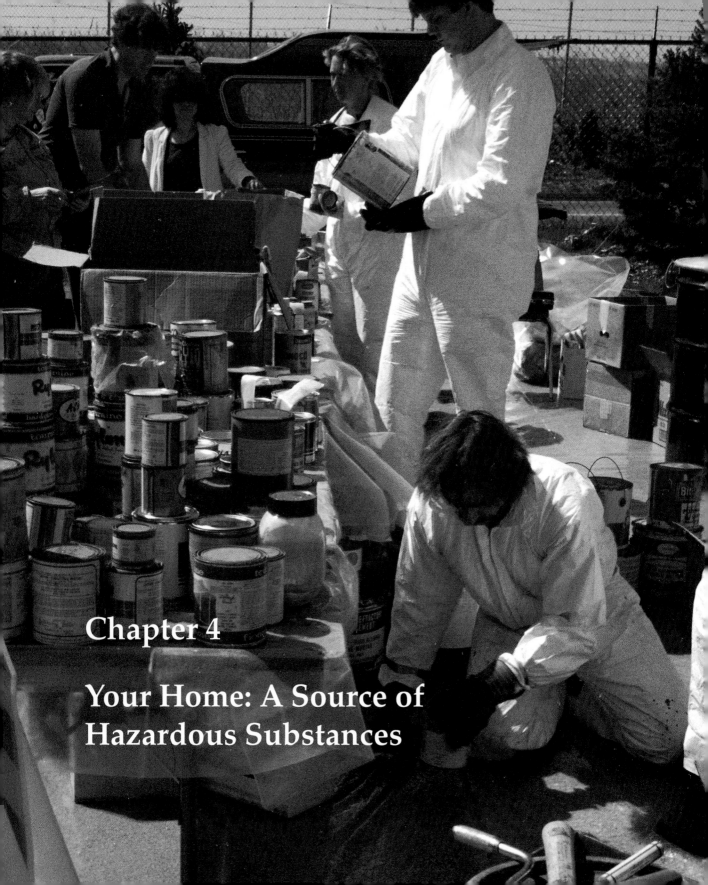

Chapter 4

Your Home: A Source of Hazardous Substances

BY FAR THE LARGEST part of hazardous waste comes from industry, but some of it comes from our homes as well. How do you and your family dispose of the things you no longer want? Most garbage your family gets rid of is probably picked up by the garbage truck each week. It goes away! Where is "away"? Most garbage is sent to the local landfill.

What about the items you pour down the drain or the toilet? They disappear! Where do they go? If you live in an urban area, they make their way to the sewage-treatment plant. If you live in a rural area, they go into the septic system on your property.

The problem is that landfills and treatment plants were not designed to handle all the modern wastes generated by today's households. Let's see how modern ways of life have given way to new waste products, by comparing life in 1900 to today.

Americans have always wanted clean homes. In 1900, brushes, mops, soap, and water were the tools. And many hours of hard work made for a clean house. Today we have special chemicals for just about every cleaning job. Powerful cleaners exist for walls, floors, furniture, wallpaper, and ovens, just to name a few. There are special disinfectants for toilets, bathtubs, and floors. Chemicals are added to toilets to keep them from getting dirty. We have replaced hard work with appliances such as carpet scrubbers and vacuum cleaners, both of which produce waste. Chemicals and machines are now doing much of the work. It saves people time and effort.

A municipal landfill holds all the trash that everyone who lives or works in a town throws away. Materials that are harmful to the environment will probably eventually leak down into the ground.

Clean Choices

One of the actions we can take is to reduce our own use of hazardous chemicals, such as some household cleaners.

There are many ways to clean different materials. Some require a lot of "elbow grease"—effort on the part of the person doing the cleaning. Others require more time. In the last decade, many chemicals have been developed to make cleaning easier and quicker.

Let's experiment with cleaning copper pennies. Compare a new penny with an older one—you can really see a difference! Your job is to clean some old pennies, to see if you can make them look new again.

You'll need catsup, vinegar, table salt, copper cleaner, a cloth rag, and four old pennies. Also, on a piece of paper, set up a chart like the one on the next page.

First, use the different materials to clean both sides of the penny. Start with the vinegar. Dip your cloth into the vinegar and rub the penny for one minute. In the correct column, write down how well it worked.

Now try using the salt and vinegar together. Dip your cloth first in the vinegar, then in the salt, and rub another penny for a minute. Did it clean the penny?

Next, dip the cloth into the catsup, and use it to rub another penny for a minute. How did this work?

Finally, use the copper cleaner, following the directions on the container. Is the penny clean now?

Record all your observations on the chart. Then fill in the other rows. This will help you compare the various characteristics of the cleaners you used. Do any of the materials you used have warnings on them? Are they dangerous to use? How should they be disposed of?

Comparing Cleaning Materials				
Cleaning Material	vinegar	vinegar & salt	catsup	copper cleaner
How well did it work?				
Was it easy to use?				
Any warning labels?				
Cost of the materials?				
How do you dispose of it?				

How do you recommend that someone clean pennies?

This activity used copper cleaners, but your household probably contains many other cleaners that have a specific purpose. When it's time to throw them away, these cleaners become hazardous waste, and the process of manufacturing them probably also produced hazardous waste.

Typical household hazardous waste. To help protect our planet, we should dispose of such products in a safe manner.

In 1900 the only way to keep a home free of insects and disease was to keep it clean. Today we use insecticides to control pests, and our medicine cabinets are bursting with pills, powders, and liquids that will cure just about anything.

What about the backyard of 1900? Yards were smaller in cities, special landscaping plants were rare, and the lawn mower was pushed with muscle power. Today our hardware stores have aisles of lawn products to kill the insects and weeds that live in our lawns. These products do the work that people did before.

FACT

Homeowners in the suburbs of North America now spread more pesticides and fertilizers per acre than U.S. farmers apply to the same amount of cropland—just to make their lawns green and their gardens abundant.

There are other items that we dispose of today that weren't available—and maybe weren't even thought of—

in 1900. They include batteries, electronic equipment, many kinds of plastics, synthetic fabrics, aerosol spray cans, fiberglass, cosmetics, pressure-treated wood, urethane finishes, and automotive products.

Our homes have become filled and surrounded with these new substances. Remember Mr. Yuk? Most youngsters first learn about hazardous household substances through warnings like this. When they see Mr. Yuk's ugly image on a product, they know they should leave it alone.

Many products found in the kitchen, basement, bathroom, and garage are potentially hazardous. Because of their chemical characteristics they could poison, corrode, burn your skin, or burst into flame. Many household cleaners, pesticides, automotive products, and painting supplies contain solvents, petroleum products, heavy metals, and toxic substances. When large amounts of these products are thrown in the trash or down the drain, they can injure people or animals or pollute water supplies.

Almost every one of the more than 150 million households in North America generates at least some household hazardous wastes. All of these materials should be handled safely to prevent any environmental or health problems. Even more important, we can all help reduce and eliminate the problem.

First, try to reduce the number of products you buy that contain hazardous substances. Whenever possible, avoid buying products that have hazardous characteristics or ingredients. Non-harmful substitutes for some of these products are listed at the end of this chapter. Some of these alternatives will require a little more time and effort on your part, but they are well worth it.

Mr. Yuk is the most commonly used poison prevention symbol in the United States. Other Poison Centers have developed their own. For information concerning poison prevention stickers, contact your local Poison Center.

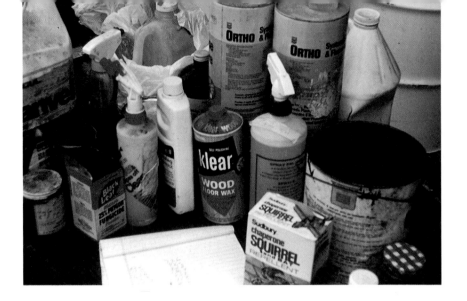

Numerous household products are designed to make life "easier" and more convenient, but getting rid of the hazardous waste associated with making and using them is not so convenient.

FACT

The average American home uses about 25 gallons (95 liters) of hazardous substances per year. Products for automobiles, household cleaners, solvents, paints, and lawn and garden chemicals are the main sources. In fact, the average home today contains more chemicals than a typical chemistry laboratory had in 1900.

Another waste-reduction technique is to purchase only as much of a harmful substance as you need at a particular time. This eliminates the need to store or dispose of the excess. It also saves money.

Your family can recycle several kinds of hazardous wastes. Used motor oil can be taken to a collection center or gasoline station. Other products can be shared with neighbors. You might have small amounts of leftover antifreeze, paint, or pesticides that someone else could use. Be certain that the products are in their original containers, with all labels still readable.

If you have exhausted all possibilities of recycling or reusing a product, it must then be disposed of properly.

Follow these rules from the EPA:

1. Read and follow label directions for use and disposal. Label warnings such as DO NOT REFILL THIS CONTAINER or DO NOT INCINERATE should always be followed for your safety and the safety of the environment.

2. Never remove labels from containers of household hazardous waste.

3. Never repackage household hazardous waste in containers that suggest the contents are edible, such as empty soft-drink bottles or plastic ice-cream buckets.

4. Never pour household hazardous waste into storm drains, streams, rivers, lakes, or on the ground.

5. Consult your local health or fire department for advice on disposing of specific household hazardous wastes.

6. Ideally, household hazardous waste should be turned over to a professional or community collection program.

Many substances such as paints, disinfectants, drain cleaners, and even hobby supplies can accumulate around a home. When such collections are thrown away, they should be taken in a special collection program that will dispose of them safely.

What's on a Label?

To protect people using cleaning products, manufacturers provide labels that have a variety of information on them. Select a cleaning product used in your home or school and, studying the label, answer the following questions.

–What is the product?

–What is the product used for?

–Where should the product be used?

–How should the product be applied?

–What are the ingredients?

–Are there any warnings or precautions you should heed?

–Where should the product be stored?

–How should the product be disposed of?

With the help of a parent, complete the same questions for some other products you find in your home. Below are some of the phrases you might see on labels.

CAUSES BURNS TO SKIN AND EYES ON CONTACT

FIRST AID INSTRUCTIONS

DANGER

KEEP OUT OF REACH OF CHILDREN

Hazard to Humans and Domestic Animals

Environmental Hazard

Eye Irritant

WARNING

Call Physician Immediately

CALL POISON CONTROL CENTER

Many trash collection companies hold special "Clean Sweep" days when customers can dispose of waste that should not be thrown into the regular trash or which cannot be recycled. Here, chemists from such a company are inspecting some of the waste turned in.

Many communities sponsor collection programs to dispose of household hazardous waste. These community collection programs are sometimes called "Clean Sweeps." Clean Sweeps provide an opportunity for citizens to remove potentially dangerous materials from their garages, basements, and storage areas. It's a much better alternative than pouring the materials down the drain or putting them in the weekly garbage.

Household hazardous wastes account for about 7 to 20 percent of the hazardous substances collected by municipal sewage-treatment plants in North America. In an average city of 1 million people, 31 tons (27.9 metric tons) of toilet-bowl cleaner and 131 tons (117.9 metric tons) of liquid household cleaners are emptied into the sewer system each year.

FACT

One of the most successful programs has been conducted by Hennepin County, Minnesota, which includes parts of Minneapolis. The program started in 1986 with 1,200 citizens participating. By 1988, the number of participants had increased to 6,500. That year the program collected 4,800 batteries, 13,750 gallons (52,250 liters) of paint, and more than 80 tons (72 metric tons) of chemicals. Batteries were sorted for recycling, some paint was donated for community use, and chemists analyzed, packaged, and labeled the chemicals for recycling facilities or waste disposal.

Another benefit of Clean Sweeps is the increased public awareness of hazardous wastes and their effects on the environment. Before Clean Sweeps take place in most communities, widespread publicity and education programs help citizens learn to recognize hazardous materials and more about the handling and disposal of them.

An Earth Experience

Home Sweet Home—Is It Safe?

*Discover what types of hazardous wastes you have in your home by completing the following investigation. Since you are searching for hazardous materials, you should complete this activity only with an adult. **DO NOT TOUCH ANY OF THE SUBSTANCES**. If you need to touch the container to see its warning, wear plastic gloves and wash your hands immediately to remove any chemicals.*

Label 4 columns on a sheet of paper with the titles shown on the next page, then list the chemicals shown.

*Now you're ready to investigate. **With an adult**, begin searching your house and garage for the materials shown in the chart. Add others if you find types of materials that are not listed. Complete the columns on the chart.*

After your search, answer the following questions:

People are more likely to support the programs that reduce the dangers of these materials when they understand how serious the hazardous-waste problem is. If your community does not sponsor Clean Sweeps or a similar program, you should contact local officials to see if one can be started. Many of the most successful Clean Sweeps in the country today started with one person's concern.

Compared with the amount of solid waste produced by a community, the hazardous waste produced by households seems small. At one landfill serving the Los Angeles, California, area, 185 tons (166.5 metric tons) of waste was sorted and 107 gallons (406.6 liters) of liquid hazardous wastes were detected. In King County, Washington, more than 33

1. *Should any of the materials be moved to a different place?*
2. *Do you plan to dispose of any of the materials?*
3. *Where would the material go if you put it in your garbage?*
4. *What is the safest way to dispose of the product?*
5. *Can you think of any alternative to using those products?*

Name of Substance	Amount	Warning on Label	Room Found In
Oil-Based Paint *Herbicide* *Insecticide* *Turpentine* *Drain Cleaner* *Gasoline* *Bleach* *Oven Cleaner* *Paint Remover* *General Cleaners* *Others*			

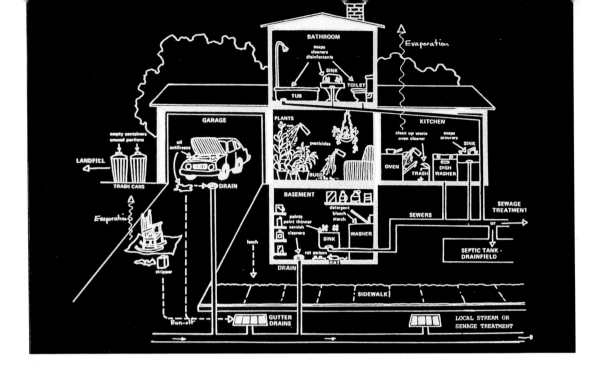

tons (29.7 metric tons) of waste were examined for household hazardous waste.

In both of these cases, hazardous material made up only about 0.1 percent of the total. However, when you consider the potential dangers of these chemicals and the tremendous amount of solid wastes generated by Canadian and United States residents, even 0.1 percent becomes very important.

The dangers of household hazardous wastes are becoming more obvious each year. Thousands of people, mostly young children, are treated each year for injuries caused by hazardous substances.

In addition to the damage they can do, it's important to reduce your family's use of chemicals for two other reasons. First, it decreases the amount of chemicals entering the environment. Second, when these products are manufactured, there are usually hazardous by-products that must be disposed of. When your family uses fewer chemicals, there's less industrial waste, too.

Alternatives to Household Hazardous Products

Product	Possible Ingredients	Problem	Disposal	Alternative
Oven Cleaner	Ammonia Potassium hydroxide Sodium hydroxide	Causes burns, toxic	Hazardous waste collection center or Clean Sweep	Dampen spill and sprinkle salt on it while oven is warm. Tough areas require baking soda and steel wool with light scrubbing
Toilet Cleaner	Hydrochloric acid Calcium hydrochlorite	Irritant, causes burns, toxic	Same as above	Baking soda, mild detergent and brush
Drain Cleaner	Hydrochloric acid Petroleum distillates	Causes burns, toxic	Same as above	Plunger, baking soda and boiling water, metal snake
Oil-based Paints	Ethylene Hydrocarbons	Flammable, toxic	Same as above	Use latex or water-based paints
Furniture Stripper	Methylene chloride, acetone, alcohols, toluene	Flammable, toxic	Same as above	Sandpaper, steel wool, heat gun
Wood Preserver	Chlorinated phenols copper, zinc, creosote	Flammable, toxic, skin irritant	Same as above	Water-based wood preservative
Copper Cleaner	Petroleum distillates	Corrosive, irritant	Same as above	Use warm vinegar and salt with a soft cloth. Rinse with water.
Pesticides — Organo-phosphates	Malathion	Toxic	Same as above	Insecticidal soap
Pesticides Chlorinated hydrocarbons	Aldrin, endrin, dieldrin, chlordane	Toxic, suspected carcinogen	Same as above	Weed garden, import predators, insecticidal soap
Pesticides Herbicides	2,4-D, glyphosate	Toxic	Same as above	Hand weeding, keep grass short
Bleach Cleaner	Hydrogen peroxide Sodium hydroxide Sodium hypochlorite	Causes burns Contact with ammonia will result in a deadly poisonous chloramine gas	Wash down drain with lots of water	Use powder -- not liquid bleach
Other Possible Products: Moth balls Aerosol cans Photo chemicals Shoe polish Mercury batteries Paint thinner Nail polish			Use according to directions, share with a neighbor, or take to a Clean Sweep	

Chapter 5

Producing the Wastes

WHAT DO PRODUCTS such as a football, fiberglass boats, cars, newspapers, plastic toys, and some farm crops have in common? First, people buy and use them. Second, in the process of making or growing them, hazardous wastes are produced.

More than 275 million tons (247.5 million metric tons) of hazardous wastes are produced each year in the United States—more than a ton for every person in the country. Imagine a truck coming to your home on the last day of the year and dropping off a ton of hazardous waste for each member of your family. It would not take long to fill up your rooms with barrels of dangerous chemicals.

Almost any large manufacturing firm produces some hazardous waste in the process of making the items it sells. Of course, chemical plants and petroleum refineries do, but so do such small businesses as auto-body repair shops, metal finishers, print shops, and dry cleaners. Farms are often sources of such chemicals as pesticides and fertilizers. These seep through the soil and enter the groundwater.

Most hazardous waste produced today results from the production of such commonly used products as plastic, medicines, paints, cosmetics, pesticides, paper, leather, and cleaners. The chemical industries are responsible for producing almost 80 percent of

Various garden products once included DDT, one of the chemicals that is most dangerous to wildlife.

hazardous waste in the United States. The petroleum refining industry is second with about 7 percent. Most of the hazardous-waste sites shown on the map on pages 72 and 73 were created by industry.

FACT

The province of Ontario, because of its strong industrial base, produces nearly half of all of Canada's hazardous waste. More than 4 million tons (3.6 million metric tons) of hazardous and liquid industrial wastes are produced each year in Ontario, about 308 pounds (140 kilograms) for every Canadian.

We will take a closer look at several of these hazardous materials, including PCBs, dioxin, arsenic, chlorinated solvents, and radioactive wastes.

Polychlorinated Biphenols (PCBs)

The PCB family of chemicals was discovered more than 100 years ago, but their use in manufacturing did not begin until 1929.

When they were first used in electrical transformers and capacitors, manufacturers found that PCBs had several qualities that made them "miracle substances." They serve as excellent electrical insulators and are extremely resistant to fire and explosions. PCBs are very stable liquid compounds that are brown in color, odorless, and, when in water, sink to the bottom. Because of these characteristics, they soon became widely used in the manufacture of other products. A partial list includes carbonless paper, plastic food containers, cosmetic creams, paint, wax, brake linings, fireproofing compounds, fluorescent light bulbs, and hydraulic fluid. The use of PCBs in this extremely wide range of products has spread them all over our planet.

It took more than 30 years of PCB use before scientists began to realize that the chemicals were a serious health and environmental problem. An incident occurred in 1968 in Japan that caught their attention—an accidental contamination of PCBs in rice oil. More than a thousand people who ate food cooked in the rice oil suffered a variety of liver and intestinal health problems, as well as birth defects.

Over the next several years, other events proved the harmful effects of PCBs. Finally, in 1977, legislation stopped production of PCBs.

It is estimated that in the 48 years that PCBs were in use 1.25 billion pounds (562.5 million kilograms) of the chemicals were manufactured in the United States. Where have the PCBs gone? Remember, PCBs are very stable and do not easily break down. So they must be somewhere.

For many years it was a common practice to discharge them directly into rivers or take them to a dump. About half of the PCBs manufactured are spread throughout the Earth's environment because of these practices. One example of where PCBs accumulate is the bottom of rivers. Scientists estimate more than 400,000 pounds (180,000 kilograms) of PCBs lie on the bottom of the Hudson River in New York. It will cost more than $7 million to clean the river and the surrounding area.

Sites where PCBs have been dumped have to be cleaned up by removing the soil and taking it away for treatment or disposal as hazardous waste.

The remaining PCBs are in equipment still being used. Many of these products are now being replaced due to their age, and the PCBs will need to be dealt with when the products are thrown away. It will be hundreds of years before these compounds can be removed from all products.

Laboratory studies have shown that PCBs are toxic. They can cause skin damage, birth defects, liver damage, and central nervous system disorders. One of the greatest concerns is that PCBs are a possible human carcinogen and can be passed on from a mother to an unborn child or to a nursing baby.

Dioxin: TCDD

The family of chemicals called dioxins is made up of 75 compounds. The most toxic of these is 2,3,7,8-TCDD. In scientific terms, the name is 2,3,7,8-tetrachlorodibenzo-paradioxin. The numbers refer to the position in which the chlorine atoms in the chemical attach to the benzene.

Considered by many to be the most toxic of all chemicals, dioxin is not intentionally produced. It has no value to industry and is not an important part of a product. Dioxins are the unavoidable by-products created in the manufacture of certain chemicals. Two such chemicals were the herbicides

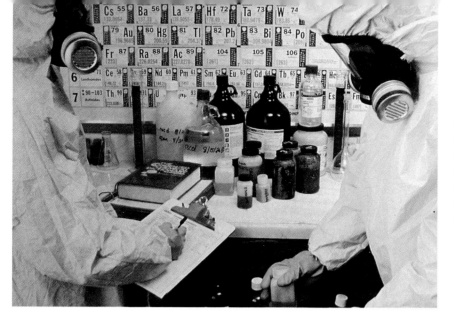

2,4,5T and silvex, used until recently in agriculture, forest management, and lawn care.

Dioxins are also contaminants in wood preservatives and Agent Orange. Agent Orange was used by American forces during the Vietnam War as a defoliant. It destroyed leaves and other plant cover that hid enemy troops. It has been estimated that more than 12 million gallons (45.6 million liters) of Agent Orange were used in Vietnam.

In recent years several other sources of dioxin have been identified. These include pulp and paper production and the incineration of certain types of plastic.

A $135-million incinerator on Long Island in New York was closed in 1980 after just one year of use, when it was found to be emitting dioxin in its smoke. There is no known way to repair such a problem.

FACT

The health effects of dioxins are highly controversial. TCDD pollution was responsible for the complete evacuation of Times Beach, Missouri. In 1984, the EPA concluded that TCDD was the "most potent animal carcinogen" it had ever tested. It may cause both immediate and long-term effects, such as skin disease, cancer, reproductive problems, and birth defects. Worldwide, there have been at least three claims among people exposed to dioxins:

1. Birth defects have increased in Vietnam because of the use of Agent Orange.

2. Many American veterans of the Vietnam War believe they and/or their children may suffer from delayed effects of exposure to Agent Orange.

3. Residents of an area in Oregon that was sprayed with 2,4,5-T and silvex suspect they have a higher rate of reproductive problems than normal.

In all of these cases, the linking of dioxin and the health problem has not been proven beyond all doubt.

Dioxin will remain in the environment even though most of the production methods that directly led to dioxins has been stopped. Studies have shown that dioxin does not readily break down into non-toxic molecules, so unless some human action is taken to dispose of them, they tend to remain in the environment. Dioxins also appear to accumulate in the fatty tissue of animals that are part of the food chain.

The EPA now requires anyone handling dioxin-containing wastes to notify the EPA before they are moved.

Arsenic

Arsenic has long been recognized as a poison. It was used in the early 1900s as a skin medicine in very small quanti-

A laboratory model of a Union Carbide combustion system used to clean up contaminated soils, including those containing dioxin. It incinerates soil faster, with less harmful emissions, than conventional systems.

ties. When a pharmacist increased the dosage by more than 20 times, women using it died. In 1903, legislation was passed banning arsenic and other poisons being used in medicines. This incident was the beginning of the science of toxicology.

Arsenic is an element that occurs naturally. It is recovered as a by-product during the processing of gold, silver, and other valuable metals. Arsenic was widely used in pesticides in the early 1900s. Today it is still used as an additive in paint, ceramics, and wallpaper, as well as in the production of electronics.

Arsenic-related deaths and illnesses caused the EPA in 1980 to list the element as a hazardous air pollutant and a carcinogen, that can cause genetic mutations.

Spray coatings are usually applied with a great deal of hazardous solvent. But a system from Union Carbide substitutes carbon dioxide, which is safer.

Chlorinated Solvents

Solvents are liquids in which other substances can be dissolved. Water is the best-known solvent. Solvents that contain chlorine can dissolve substances that water cannot, therefore the use of chlorinated solvents is growing. They are used for industrial cleaners, fire extinguishers, paint removers and thinners, computer and microchip production, and in the dry-cleaning process. Solvents made by the petroleum industry include paint, polish, glue, and adhesives such as tape.

To some degree, chlorinated solvents are poisonous. Long exposure can cause damage to the central nervous system, kidneys, and liver. Many chlorinated solvents are also proven or suspected carcinogens.

Many drinking wells in the United States, Great Britain, and the Netherlands have been closed because of the improper disposal of chlorinated solvents nearby.

Radioactive Wastes

The accident at Chernobyl drew world attention to one of the serious dangers of nuclear power. Another danger—the production of radioactive wastes—is occurring every day at nuclear power plants around the world.

The atomic age started in 1945. Atomic bombs developed by the United States were dropped on two cities in Japan to end World War II. Atomic energy's destructive power was clearly proven, but many felt that it could have positive uses, too. A process using nuclear energy to create electricity was developed. At the time, scientists believed that they would be able to discover a way to safely dispose of the wastes. Today, almost 50 years later, scientists are still searching for a safe disposal method.

Radioactive wastes remain hazardous for at least 100,000 years, sometimes much longer. No one is sure how much waste exists, but it can be found in many places. Radioactive wastes are stored in an underground tank in Idaho, in pools in Maine, in warehouses in California, in shallow ditches in Tennessee, and elsewhere throughout the world.

There are two major sources of radioactive wastes. Some comes from the production of nuclear weapons, and more is produced by nuclear reactors at power plants. When fuel rods, like those shown on page 62, are used up, they must be disposed of. The United States has about 110 nuclear reactors, producing more than 30 tons (27 metric tons) of radioactive wastes each year. Some of this waste will

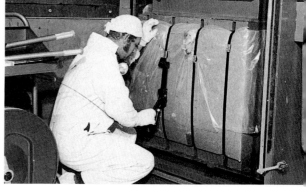

remain dangerous for more than a *million* years.

Currently, radioactive wastes are being stored at each reactor in pools of water or steel casks. But some of these containers are leaking. They were designed to last 50 years, but they are holding wastes that will be dangerous for thousands and thousands of years. Yet, how can radioactive wastes be stored safely for 100,000 years? No one can answer that. This raises a serious question: Should we continue to build more nuclear power plants before the disposal issue is solved?

The United States has made little progress in finding a safe final resting place for radioactive material. Many underground sites have been explored, and a site in Nevada was selected as a storage area. But the state of Nevada has delayed work at the site by taking the issue to court to protest it. The earliest this facility could begin accepting wastes would be 2010. But for now, "temporary" on-site storage is the method of handling radioactive waste.

In Oberrothenbach, Germany—formerly East Germany—the entire area is contaminated by very high levels of radioactivity and arsenic from uranium deposits mined by the Soviet Union. The wastes form a lake that is linked to many cases of cancer.

Radioactive and chemical wastes can, when apparently disposed of, travel hundreds of miles by air or water. Many times they seem to disappear, but they never truly go "away."

Wastes from nuclear processing plants (left) *must be buried in the earth, probably forever, because they are so hazardous to human health and the environment. Even small quantities of nuclear waste* (right), *such as from a hospital, must be packaged and handled with great care.*

Great Lakes Areas of Concern:

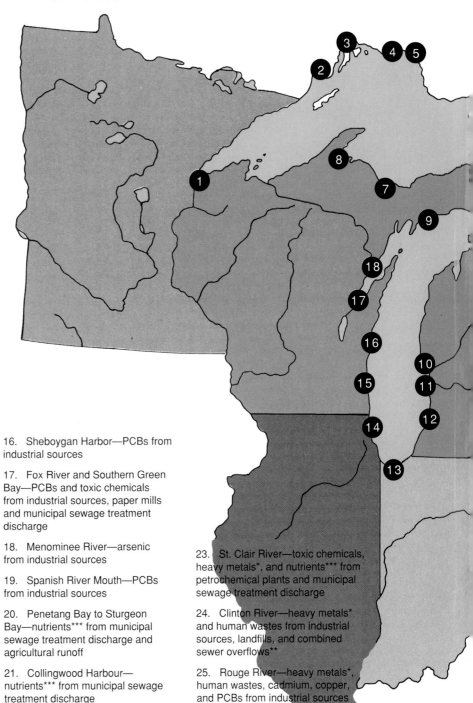

1.   St. Louis River—PCBs from steel mills and municipal sewage treatment discharge

2.   Thunder Bay—mercury and heavy metals* from paper mills

3.   Nipigon Bay—mercury and toxic chemicals from paper mills and municipal sewage treatment discharge

4.   Jackfish Bay—toxic chemicals from paper mills

5.   Peninsula Harbour—mercury and PCBs from paper mills and municipal sewage treatment discharge

6.   St. Marys River—heavy metals* and PCBs from industrial sources

7.   Deer Lake, Carp Creek, and Carp River—mercury from iron companies and sewage treatment discharge

8.   Torch Lake—toxic chemicals from industrial sources and copper ore mining

9.   Manistique River—PCBs and heavy metals* from sewage treatment discharge and paper mills

10.   White Lake—PCBs and toxic chemicals in the groundwater from chemical and leather companies

11.   Muskegon Lake—mercury and heavy metals* from chemical and industrial sources, municipal sewage treatment discharge and combined sewer overflows**

12.   Kalamazoo River—PCBs from industrial sources

13.   Grand Calumet River and Indiana Harbor Canal—PCBs and heavy metals* from industrial sources and combined sewer overflows**

14.   Waukegan Harbor—PCBs from industrial sources

15.   Milwaukee Estuary—contaminated sediments, human wastes, PCBs and DDT from municipal sewage treatment discharge, industrial sources, and combined sewer overflows**

16.   Sheboygan Harbor—PCBs from industrial sources

17.   Fox River and Southern Green Bay—PCBs and toxic chemicals from industrial sources, paper mills and municipal sewage treatment discharge

18.   Menominee River—arsenic from industrial sources

19.   Spanish River Mouth—PCBs from industrial sources

20.   Penetang Bay to Sturgeon Bay—nutrients*** from municipal sewage treatment discharge and agricultural runoff

21.   Collingwood Harbour—nutrients*** from municipal sewage treatment discharge

22.   Saginaw River and Saginaw Bay—PCBs, heavy metals* and nutrients*** from industrial sources, municipal sewage treatment discharge and agricultural runoff

23.   St. Clair River—toxic chemicals, heavy metals*, and nutrients*** from petrochemical plants and municipal sewage treatment discharge

24.   Clinton River—heavy metals* and human wastes from industrial sources, landfills, and combined sewer overflows**

25.   Rouge River—heavy metals*, human wastes, cadmium, copper, and PCBs from industrial sources and combined sewer overflows**

26.   Detroit River—heavy metals*, human wastes, and PCBs from municipal and industrial sources, and combined sewer overflows**

Pollution Problems and Sources

The Areas of Concern are 43 heavily polluted sites in the Great Lakes. Types of pollutants found at each, and their sources, are listed below.

The state or province where each site is located is responsible for its cleanup effort. Different methods for measuring the seriousness of the problem are used by each government agency, so not all sites are equally harmful to human health and the environment. At all areas, however, Remedial Action Plans to guide specific cleanup projects are being prepared.

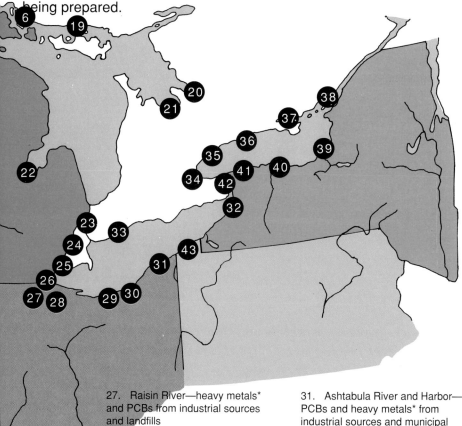

35. Toronto Waterfront—PCBs, human wastes, insecticide, and nutrients*** from industrial sources and combined sewer overflows**

36. Port Hope—radioactive materials and heavy metals* from a uranium refinery and industrial sources

37. Bay of Quinte—nutrients*** from municipal sewage treatment discharge and agricultural runoff

38. St. Lawrence River—PCBs, mercury, nutrients*** and human wastes from industrial sources, chemical plants and municipal sewage treatment discharge

39. Oswego River—PCBs, insecticides, and heavy metals* from industrial sources and combined sewer overflows**

40. Rochester Embayment—heavy metals* and toxic chemicals from industrial sources, municipal sewage treatment discharge and combined sewer overflows**

41. Eighteen Mile Creek—heavy metals* and toxic chemicals from industrial sources and municipal sewage treatment discharge

42. Niagara River—heavy metals* and toxic chemicals from petro-chemical plants and landfills

43. Erie Harbor—heavy metals*, PCBs and pesticides from industrial sources and municipal sewage treatment discharge

27. Raisin River—heavy metals* and PCBs from industrial sources and landfills

28. Maumee River—PCBs and heavy metals* from agricultural runoff, landfills, industrial sources and combined sewer overflows**

29. Black River—heavy metals* from municipal sewage treatment discharge, industrial sources, and combined sewer overflows**

30. Cuyahoga River—heavy metals* and human wastes from steel mills, chemical plants, and combined sewer overflows**

31. Ashtabula River and Harbor—PCBs and heavy metals* from industrial sources and municipal sewage treatment discharge plants

32. Buffalo River—PCBs and heavy metals* from industrial sources and combined sewer overflows**

33. Wheatley Harbour—human wastes and nutrients*** from food processing operations

34. Hamilton Harbour—nutrients*** and heavy metals* from industrial sources, municipal sewage treatment discharge, and combined sewer overflows**

NOTES:

*heavy metals: metals, such as arsenic, cadmium, chromium, copper, lead, and mercury, that cause human health problems.

**combined sewer overflows: occurs when the overflow from combined sewer and storm sewer systems is released into waterways following heavy rains.

***nutrients: pollutants, such as phosphorus and nitrogen, that cause excessive algal growth and low oxygen in water.

73

Chapter 6

There Is No "Away" — Disposing of Hazardous Wastes

ACROSS THE UNITED STATES, more than 30,000 potentially contaminated sites have been identified. Each of them may threaten human health. These sites may contaminate groundwater, lead to a dangerous fire or explosion, kill wildlife, or cause health problems in people living nearby. Almost eight out of every ten North Americans live near a hazardous-waste site.

Most abandoned waste sites are in some way connected to the chemical and petroleum industries. Some were city landfills that became hazardous sites because so much of the wastes from small companies and households turned out to be hazardous. Several hundred contaminated sites were the result of accidents or spills. Unfortunately, many of these sites are located in wetlands and floodplains (areas that take the overflow from rivers). These areas were once thought to be worthless, so people figured they might as well dump things in them.

Most hazardous waste is still just dumped or buried. It is the least expensive method, but the most dangerous. Land disposal sites have evolved over the years from open dumps to sanitary landfills to secured landfills.

Surface Disposal

Open Dumps. Until 1975, hazardous wastes were just mixed in with the rest of the country's 6 billion pounds (2.7 billion kilograms) of garbage each year. And almost all of it was disposed of in open dumps. Open dumps were located just about anywhere—along rivers, in wetlands, in abandoned gravel pits, or in almost any field. These dumps received all types of hazardous waste, and today many of

At Colorado's Rocky Mountain Arsenal, a 93-acre (37-hectare) sludge pond contains chemical wastes from both the U.S. Army and Shell Oil Company. As the liquid evaporated, it left concentrated contamination behind.

them require expensive cleanup efforts.

Near Gray, Maine, many residents complained of headaches, dizziness, and burning eyes. A young girl developed severe bladder and liver disorders. These problems prompted local officials to investigate a nearby open dump site. They found thousands of gallons of oil and chemicals on the 7-acre (2.8-hectare) site, along with hundreds of drums full of hazardous wastes and an old incinerator. Sixteen wells and a large area of land around the dump were contaminated by the wastes.

The waste-collection business had been operating there for years, and the people who drank and bathed in the contaminated water feared their health might be in danger. The residents started drinking bottled water, while the area was studied extensively.

During the next ten years, the drums and liquids were removed, 12,000 cubic yards (9,174 cubic meters) of contaminated soil were treated, and groundwater treatment was started. Finally, the area was planted over as a meadow.

Some types of dump sites are not usually considered

hazardous, because they hold products that we commonly use. But when piles of old cars, refrigerators, and other appliances catch on fire, they can release harmful chemicals into the ground and air.

A major environmental disaster took place in Hagersville, Ontario, in early 1990, when a tire pile the size of 18 football fields caught on fire. The 17-day blaze melted many of the 14 million tires on the site, releasing toxic air emissions and up to 28 million gallons (106 million liters) of oil, as well as many other toxic chemicals. The water sprayed on the fire carried the chemicals with it into the ground, contaminating the soil to a depth of about 10 feet (3 meters). A nearby creek held more than 50 times the standard level of benzene.

Heavy black smoke caused hundreds of residents to evacuate the area, and five families had to leave their homes permanently after the fire.

Workers pumped water onto the site, in order to keep the oil floating above ground level, rather than seeping into the soil. The oil was then collected and disposed of at a hazardous-waste facility. Area groundwater supplies are still monitored, to ensure that drinking water remains safe.

These are stories that will likely be repeated many times in the future.

The fire in the tire dump at Hagersville, Ontario, burned for 17 days, and produced huge quantities of liquid hazardous waste that had to be collected.

FACT

In the province of Ontario alone, there are an estimated 3,000 unrecorded waste-disposal sites—places where people illegally or thoughtlessly just took their waste and dumped it. Some of the sites contain hazardous waste.

Sanitary Landfills. Open dumps were prohibited in the mid-1970s and replaced by sanitary landfills, which most lawmakers felt were safer.

Unlike open dumps, sanitary landfills have operating requirements and construction-design rules, and are monitored for pollution. States require landfills to have some type of liner to prevent polluted liquids, called leachate, from seeping into the groundwater or nearby streams. The source of the liquid leachate in a landfill is either precip-itation that trickles through the waste or the waste material itself. The liners, usually a layer of plastic or compacted clay, work temporarily, but over enough time, all will leak, allowing the leachate to seep into the surrounding ground.

Today, sanitary landfills can still receive most household hazardous wastes but cannot accept hazardous wastes from most industries and commercial generators. These wastes go to hazardous-waste landfills.

Hazardous-Waste Landfills. The greatest difference be-tween a sanitary landfill and a hazardous-waste landfill, also called a secured landfill, is the level of protection to prevent leaking. New hazardous-waste landfills are usually located in rural areas. The best soil is clay and the site cannot be located on a floodplain.

The landfills are carefully designed with several layers of compacted clay and thick plastic liners to prevent the leachate from escaping. Leachate gathers at the bottom of the landfill where it is collected and treated to make it safer. Monitoring wells are installed to detect any leaking. Water samples from these wells are collected and tested on a regular basis.

Each secured landfill is licensed and regulated, because the amount of material that can be put in each landfill is limited. When a landfill is filled with waste to capacity, it is covered by another layer of plastic, compacted clay, and some type of vegetation. Unlike municipal landfills, which can be turned into parkland, land containing a hazardous-waste landfill may not be used for any other type of development.

The construction and operation of a hazardous-waste landfill is very expensive. Each will need to be monitored for hundreds of years, because, again, all will eventually leak. It is simply a matter of time, according to the EPA, the Na-

In constructing this hazardous-waste landfill, a synthetic liner is installed to prevent hazardous leachate from leaking into the surrounding environment.

tional Academy of Sciences, and the Congressional Office of Technology Assessment. At some point, action will have to be taken to control the leakage.

Few people want landfills near them. This situation is called the "NIMBY" or "Not In My Backyard" syndrome. North Carolina, South Carolina, and Alabama tried to prohibit accepting hazardous waste from other states. However, in June 1991 the U.S. Supreme Court ruled that hazardous waste was a normal product of interstate commerce and thus could not be prohibited.

Some community groups feel that legal action within states will not only keep hazardous wastes out of their area, but will have the additional benefit of making it so difficult for companies to dispose of hazardous materials that they will stop generating the wastes. Instead of NIMBY, their slogan is NIABY—"Not in anyone's backyard!"

In the future, hazardous-waste landfills will be expensive to construct and it will be increasingly difficult to find a place to build them. Industries will need another solution.

Some toxic-waste disposal firms are negotiating with Indian tribes to build waste sites on their reservations. Since state laws do not apply on reservations, the companies can avoid the tough regulations and restrictions. And they are willing to pay the tribes millions of dollars to do so. The promise of jobs on reservations, where unemployment is high, is appealing to some of the tribes. Other Native Americans, though, feel that no amount of money is worth harming their land.

For example, Waste-Tech, a subsidiary of Amoco Oil Company, signed a contract in 1990 with the Kaw Indians of northern Oklahoma to build an incinerator and landfill on their reservation. However, they canceled the contract in 1991. Navajos at Dilkon, Arizona, turned down a similar offer from Waste-Tech in 1989.

We know that even hazardous-waste sites are unable to contain dangerous wastes for long periods of time. They are, at best, just a temporary storage area for hazardous wastes.

The cost of landfill disposal was once less than $10 per ton (0.9 metric ton) of hazardous waste. Today, with all the controls and technological equipment needed to make hazardous-waste disposal safer, the cost is anywhere from $250 to $1,000 per ton.

FACT

Deep Well Injection

The oil industry has disposed of its waste in deep wells for more than fifty years. Now other industries are using this method. Wells, or injection tubes, are drilled thousands of feet into the Earth through layers of dense clay and into sand or porous rock formations. Pressurized liquid wastes are then pumped into the well down to the porous rock layer where, in theory, they will be stored forever.

Almost 50 percent of all hazardous wastes produced in the United States are disposed of in deep wells. Those in favor of this method say that between 25 and 50 percent of the land in the United States could support deep well injection systems. But there are great risks.

The danger of contaminating groundwater used for drinking is always present because liquids flow through porous rock. Wastes leaking from the well could contaminate other layers of the Earth. The path these chemicals will take under the surface cannot be predicted, and they may cause trouble many years from now.

Not all states permit deep well injection. The dangerous possibility that wastes disposed of in this way will move through the underground rocks makes deep wells a poor choice for hazardous-waste disposal.

Surface Impoundments

A surface impoundment may look invitingly like a swimming pool, but it is filled with hazardous materials.

Surface impoundments are waste areas constructed like swimming pools. They are used to hold liquid hazardous wastes for years, but like swimming pools, they can leak. Many of them are slowly releasing harmful chemicals into the soil and groundwater.

Some surface impoundments, however, are using modern technology to make them safer. One industry in Alabama has a surface impoundment larger than a football field. It's equipped with a clay base, a plastic liner, and several leak-detection systems. Still, like landfills, no one knows how to design a surface impoundment that won't eventually leak.

Treating Waste to Make It Safer

Because so much public attention is given to burying hazardous wastes, industries have turned to using various methods to either treat the hazardous waste or recycle the material. The goals of waste treatment are either to reduce the amount of hazardous-waste materials or to convert the materials into non-hazardous wastes. Some treatment methods separate the waste materials involved, so that at least some of the hazardous wastes can be recycled or reused.

Biological Treatment. Biological treatment uses living organisms to decompose different types of organic hazardous wastes. This can take place in waste stabilization ponds, in aerated lagoons, or by land farming.

Waste stabilization ponds are large, shallow ponds designed to give different organisms a chance to decompose certain types of hazardous-waste materials. The tiny, bacteria-like organisms eat the hazardous materials and break them into harmless substances.

Aerated lagoons operate in the same way, but oxygen is also added to the water to provide more oxygen to the organisms.

Land farming is a type of biological treatment in which certain wastes are spread on the land and mixed into the soil. The wastes are supposed to be decomposed in the soil by the organisms living there. Yet, problems can arise when the harmful chemicals seep into the groundwater or evaporate into the air before they are decomposed.

A unit used for the biological treatment of hazardous chemical wastes uses microorganisms to break down leachate and other liquid materials so that the water content can be sent directly to a wastewater-treatment plant.

Biological treatment is especially effective with sludge from petroleum refineries and wastes from sewage-treatment plants. Caution must be used with other wastes because heavy metals and other non-biodegradable materials might accumulate in the ponds or the fields.

Chemical Treatment. Chemical treatment reduces the volume and strength of hazardous wastes. Four different methods are used.

Neutralization has been commonly used to change harmful acids into harmless substances. Acids have a very low pH (below 2.5). Lime, a base with a high pH, is added to neutralize the material, making it safe to dispose of.

Changing the pH in a process called *precipitation* also allows the removal of toxic metals. In precipitation, certain dissolved metals may be removed after they have been caused to solidify by changing their pH or temperature. This process has been used in the metal-finishing industries.

Stabilization and *solidification* are treatments that make hazardous wastes less likely to be released into the environment. Stabilization makes the waste less able to be broken down into a form that could easily enter the environment. The solidification process turns liquid hazardous wastes into solids. Engineers and scientists mix hazardous wastes with such materials as

One type of recovery drum used to move hazardous materials contains a liquid base that will neutralize dangerous acid. That makes it less likely to cause problems while being transported.

Contaminated soil can be turned into solid glass by a vitrification process. Once hardened, the lump can be removed as a whole, without danger to the rest of the environment.

cement or fly ash. However, no one is yet certain that the hardened waste material will not break down over time.

A new solidification method is called *in situ vitrification*. Soil in a contaminated area is superheated with electricity, becoming so hot that it turns into glass. This way, hazardous materials can be treated without removing them from the waste site, eliminating the chance of spills. However, dangerous gases are given off during the process.

A site in Washington, with soil contaminated by a nuclear weapons facility, was treated in this way. Researchers are doing tests to learn if this treatment can be used successfully in many other areas, too.

Taking the Hazard Out of Wastes

When hazardous wastes go through the process of neutraliza-tion, they are changed into safer chemicals. One of the common methods of neutralization is to change the pH, or the level of acidity, of the waste. Though their level of toxicity doesn't change, the hazardous characteristics of the acid are decreased, so they can be disposed of with less harm.

Let's pretend that lemon juice is a dangerous acid that needs to be neutralized. Use acid-measuring paper to get a reading on how acidic it is; you can obtain acid-measuring paper at a scientific supply store. Put ¼ teaspoon of lime (from a garden shop) into 1 cup (235 milliliters) of lemon juice. Take another reading with the acid-measuring paper. Then continue to add small amounts of lime until the solution is about 7, or neutral. It can now be dis-posed of more safely.

Some people spread lime on their lawns to "sweeten" them. When the soil becomes too acidic, grasses and many flowering plants do not grow well. The lime neutralizes the acid and the lawns again become green and lush.

Physical Treatment. Another way to handle some hazard-ous chemicals is to separate them from other materials with which they have been combined. In this way, the amount of hazardous waste is reduced. Sometimes the wastes can even be recycled.

Air stripping is used to remove hazardous chemicals that are easily vaporized. Air is forced through the contaminated liquid, vaporizing certain hazardous chemicals. The mixture

of air and chemicals that results from air stripping must be further treated before it is released.

In *carbon absorption*, particles of carbon are specially treated and put into tanks of the liquid mixture to be separated. The hazardous chemicals are attracted to the carbon particles and are removed from the liquid. The contaminated carbon must then be disposed of or cleaned and recycled.

Without warning, the residents of Battle Creek, Michigan, had to become familiar with these processes. In 1981, nearly one hundred area wells were found to be contaminated with chemicals called volatile organic compounds (VOCs), which are suspected carcinogens. In a cleanup process expected to last until 1995, the contaminated groundwater is pumped first through an air stripper and then through a carbon absorption system.

Water is pumped into a tower that has a high-powered fan at the bottom. When air is forced through the water, it strips the VOCs from the water. Then the contaminated air is cleaned when it is forced through tanks containing activated carbon that removes the VOCs from the air.

Some hazardous waste can be incinerated (left) in incinerators that collect hazardous particles from the smoke. A portable incinerator (right) can be taken to a hazardous-waste site so that material can be burned without having to transport it first.

A facility for treating contaminated liquid waste (left) *evaporates the waste to concentrate the contaminants and then chemically combines them with oxygen, leaving reusable water. Contaminated soil can be cleaned up with equipment* (right) *that evaporates the organic compounds from the soil. The equipment can be moved to major hazardous-waste sites for long-term use.*

Thermal Treatment or Incineration. A high-temperature incinerator is very different from a typical incinerator. It reaches extremely high temperatures (1100-2200 degrees F., or 593-1204 degrees C) to destroy molecules of hazardous waste. Incineration has two distinct advantages. It greatly reduces the volume of waste and the heat can also be used to generate steam for heating buildings.

Incineration does have drawbacks, however. The EPA requires 99.99 percent of the molecules of the hazardous chemicals to be destroyed. Therefore, a small amount is left to enter the air or remain in the ash. Expensive air-pollution equipment must be added to capture the emissions. Those captured emissions and the remaining ash still must be disposed of in a hazardous-waste landfill. Also, incinerators must be monitored closely to ensure they are functioning at a high level of efficiency. If they burn at less than full efficiency, they might leave too much of the hazardous chemical intact.

Another problem is that combustion may create new compounds that are even more dangerous. So far, there is no good solution to this problem.

Incineration cannot be used to treat some types of hazardous wastes. For example, elements such as arsenic and lead aren't destroyed by high temperatures.

Constructing and operating incinerators is very expensive. In addition, incinerators have been nicknamed "landfills in the sky," and, just like landfills, sites for incinerators are difficult to find. Many people are concerned that incinerators are not safe, and they don't want more built.

Special New Techniques. Scientists are working in laboratories around the world to develop new techniques that

Solvents are powerful, often hazardous, chemicals used to dissolve other materials. In the boilers shown here, however, waste solvents can be used as fuels to make cement and other products safely. The process also saves fossil fuels.

will reduce the world's hazardous waste. These methods have included the development of "superbugs" which speed up the breakdown of dangerous chemicals.

Tiny microbes, which are often called "bugs," have been used for years to help break down sewage. The high cost of hazardous-waste disposal and other treatment methods has provided a new incentive for the use of bugs.

Scientists are trying thousands of different superbugs, in some cases, with great success. One company has successfully used microbes to break down diesel fuel that was contaminating soil and groundwater. This method is expected to save both time and money. Other superbugs are being tested on PCBs, solvents, dioxin, and heavy metals.

Recycling and Waste Exchange. One company's hazardous waste may be another's resource. The EPA estimates that about 20 percent of hazardous wastes could be reused or recycled. To implement waste exchange, an industry can list in a catalog any waste materials that may provide a resource for another company.

For example, the DuPont Company used to dispose of 8 million pounds (3.6 million kilograms) of a chemical by-product called hexamethyleneimine (HMI), used in making nylon. Now HMI is being sold and used as a resource in the drugs and coatings industries.

With disposal costs continuing to rise, hazardous-waste recycling is being considered by more companies. There is a barrier to the success of such recycling, however. Many companies make products containing "secret" ingredients. They're afraid that if they let another company recycle their waste, their secrets will be discovered.

Exporting Love Canal

As hazardous-waste disposal becomes more expensive, the laws and regulations surrounding it are also becoming more complex and difficult to follow. As a result, many American and European companies dispose of hazardous wastes elsewhere around the world. Third World countries, which have fewer regulations and poor enforcement of disposal laws, are becoming the Love Canals of the future.

In 1980, only 12 companies notified the EPA of their "intent to ship" hazardous wastes to a foreign country. This notification is required by law, but the EPA cannot stop the shipments. The EPA estimated that 100,000 tons (90,000 metric tons) of hazardous wastes were shipped to other countries in 1987. By 1989 the figure was 140,000 tons (126,000 metric tons). Many government officials believe these figures are much lower than the actual amount being shipped.

In 1989, 140,000 tons (126,000 metric tons) of hazardous waste were shipped from the United States to other countries. About 85 percent of that waste was transported across the border into Canada for disposal.

FACT

One reason companies ship waste away is to save on future responsibility. If a company disposes of a chemical in a United States landfill, and that landfill leaks twenty years later, the company must pay for the cleanup. There is no further responsibility after shipping wastes abroad.

The Khian Sea *was a hazardous-waste site in search of a place to land its burdensome cargo for more than two years. This photo was taken after the ship's name was changed to the* Pelicano.

The Ship of Wastes

The city of Philadelphia paid a company to dispose of the hazardous wastes produced by the city's incinerators. In 1986, a total of 13,000 tons (11,700 metric tons) of ash were loaded on a ship called the *Khian Sea*. The ash contained levels of dioxin higher than those found in the soil at Times Beach, Missouri. In June 1986, the *Khian Sea* started its voyage over the oceans looking for a place to dispose of the toxic ash. It spent twenty-seven months at sea, stopping at Panama, Haiti, Honduras, Bermuda, Africa, and the Bahamas in its attempts to unload the toxic ash, labeled "fertilizer ash." While at a port in Haiti, one crew member even ate some of the ash to show how safe it was. He failed to convince the local officials to accept the material, but the ship did manage to dump about 3,000 tons (2,700 metric tons) of the ash at the edge of the ocean near a Haitian port before being sent away.

The ship eventually returned to Philadelphia with its cargo, only to be turned away by the very city that had created the waste. With the ship showing signs of rusting, it departed again with a new name—the *Felicia*. It reached the Philippines where it was again turned away.

After another name change, the ship—now called the *Pelicano*—docked at Singapore. The cargo of hazardous wastes had disappeared. No one on board would say what happened to the material other than that it was unloaded at an unnamed port. Some environmental groups think the waste was dumped into the ocean.

Some of the ash that the *Khian Sea* left in Haiti made its way back to the United States in late 1990, when a Haitian environmental group placed small portions of the waste into envelopes and put them in the mail. About 250 envelopes were sent to Philadelphia Mayor W. Wilson Goode, and another 250 went to the head of the EPA, William Reilly. Each envelope was labeled: "Contains Philadelphia Waste. Return to sender. Delivered three years ago. Mislabeled as fertilizer." There was no return address.

FACT

The story of the *Khian Sea* or the *Felicia* or the *Pelicano* is becoming more common. The growing global concern about shipping toxic wastes caused 117 nations to send representatives to Basel, Switzerland, in 1989. This was the site of the spill into the Rhine River. The goal of the representatives was to reach a treaty on the export of hazardous wastes.

The agreement that was reached does not call for a ban on exporting toxic wastes. Nor does it ban nations from sending wastes to countries that have lower standards for

Midnight dumping, or the illegal disposal of hazardous waste, may consist of quietly rolling drums off a truck in the night. Each drum of waste found where it doesn't belong must be investigated.

disposal than their own.

But the Basel Convention does set down several rules to be followed. It requires accurate labeling of wastes, and the receiving country must approve the shipment before it can be sent. The treaty is a beginning, but future agreements will need to be more stringent to stop the global exporting of "Love Canals."

Midnight Dumping

Because getting rid of hazardous chemicals in an approved manner can be expensive, some companies choose to dump their waste illegally. They may pour barrels of wastes into sewer systems. Or they may take drums full of hazardous materials to abandoned warehouses or remote fields and just leave them there. Other wastes are dumped in ditches or buried in remote areas. People who illegally dispose of hazardous chemicals by such methods are called "midnight dumpers."

Midnight dumping can occur anywhere.

Late one evening on a lonely North Carolina highway, a truck was traveling slowly. The driver of a car behind the truck honked his horn, trying to get the truck driver's attention. He wanted to let the driver know that his truck was leaking an oil-like substance along the edge of the road.

But the truck didn't stop and, eventually, the driver of

the car gave up trying to be a good citizen.

The next day, a foul smell caused local residents to contact environmental officials, who investigated the roadway and ditches. They found dangerously high levels of PCBs along more than 200 miles (322 kilometers) of roadway. A reward was offered for information on who dumped the hazardous liquid. Finally, the driver and his truck were found, and the driver was arrested.

In Wisconsin, an anonymous call on the state's Spills Hotline alerted officials to a company's plan to bury drums of wastes behind their plant. The state investigators secretly took pictures as the company's workers unloaded more than one hundred barrels into trenches behind the building. The photos were all that was needed to force the company to clean up the area. The materials in the drums were high in lead and chromium, two chemicals that can cause serious health effects in humans.

Without that call from the concerned citizen, the illegal dumping would probably have been successful.

EPA officials have found abandoned barrels all across the nation. They have been discovered in vacant houses in Louisiana, on the medians of highways in New Jersey, and in the forests of South Carolina. Only greater enforcement and reporting by educated citizens will reduce the amount of "midnight dumping."

Illegal dumping of hazardous wastes is certainly a serious problem. The United States government has responded by passing laws that not only regulate the use and disposal of hazardous waste, but also set up some guidelines for cleaning up the mess. And, as you'll see in the next chapter, many companies are becoming more responsible.

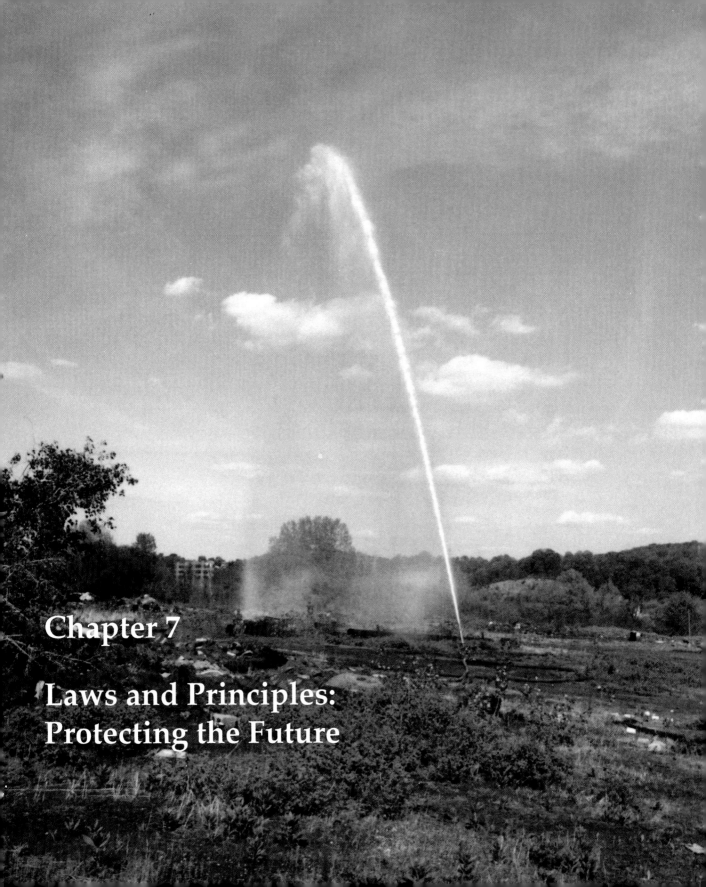

Chapter 7

Laws and Principles: Protecting the Future

IN THE EARLY 1970s, the United States had successfully completed several landings on the moon. Many people were amazed by that technological accomplishment, but some of them began to wonder, "If we can go to the moon, why can't we solve our hazardous-waste problem?"

Few people knew of the scope of the hazardous-waste problem in the early 1970s, but it was soon to become a national and even global issue.

Up to that time, hazardous wastes were discarded at the lowest possible cost—sometimes in a legal manner, and sometimes not. There were few rules controlling the disposal of hazardous wastes, so numerous problems developed. Once the dangers were realized, many hazardous-waste disposal sites needed immediate cleanup to keep down the dangerous health effects. Still, little was known about how to clean up these sites or use hazardous materials safely and effectively. So federal and state governments began to develop laws and regulations in an attempt to control them.

Early Laws

The first national law to improve the management of hazardous wastes was the Resources Conservation and Recovery Act (RCRA) of 1976. It helped identify hazardous wastes, listed guidelines for using and treating them, and developed a method to track the hazardous wastes from the place where they are created to their eventual disposal (from "the cradle to the grave").

Also passed in 1976 was the Toxic Substances Control Act. It allowed the EPA to monitor production, use, and health and environmental effects of various chemicals.

Superfund

The discovery of the dangers at Love Canal led the United States government to develop a law that would protect citizens against the dangers presented by hazardous-waste sites across the country. The law, nicknamed "Superfund," is officially called the Comprehensive Environmental Response, Compensation, and Liability Act of 1980. It was designed to deal with the tremendous task of cleaning up hundreds of known contaminated sites.

Superfund has many key points. Mainly, the law:

1.   Developed the National Priorities List (NPL), a list of priority sites that present the most serious threat to human health and the environment.

2.   Made the polluter pay for cleanups when possible.

3.   Established a $1.6-billion Superfund to respond to emergency situations and start cleanup of other sites.

4.   Encouraged new research to find ways to reduce, treat, and dispose of hazardous waste.

Because the Superfund law requires the owners, operators, and customers of a disposal facility or spill site to pay for any short- or long-term cleanup costs or property damage, many citizens applauded the law. The message it sent was simple: "You are responsible for your waste forever."

The EPA judges hazardous-waste sites against a rating system that uses all available information about how contaminated a site is and what its effects might be on human health. Sites that present the greatest dangers are included on the NPL. In 1982, the NPL contained only 115 sites. By 1990, the list had grown to 1,207 sites.

States that have a large number of chemical plants or industries usually have the greatest number of NPL sites.

CT	15
DE	20
MD	10
MA	25
NH	10
NJ	109
RI	11
VT	8
DC	0

The number of approved and proposed Super-fund hazardous-waste sites in each state as of 1991

New Jersey has 109 sites—more than any other state in the country. The other states in the top five include Pennsylvania, California, New York, and Michigan.

In order for a hazardous-waste disposal site to be declared a Superfund site, the reported site must be studied carefully. Researchers need to learn about the type and amount of the wastes discarded on the site, the actual dangers to the public and the environment that are presented, and who is responsible. Further studies reveal how to treat and clean up the mess.

An emergency cleanup or waste removal could be completed at any point in this process, if quick action is necessary to protect human safety.

This Superfund site in Michigan spontaneously caught fire every spring for three years because of large amounts of methane gas at the site. During the cleanup, a trench was dug to vent the methane.

The Superfund Score: Good or Bad?

In the first six years of the Superfund program, more than 25,000 waste sites were reported to the EPA. Over 20,000 sites received background searches and investigations were completed at 6,484. A total of 888 sites were listed on the NPL, and emergency waste-removal actions were completed at 716 sites.

The Superfund program also helped establish new methods to treat and dispose of hazardous wastes. The numbers seem impressive; however, progress has been slow.

The legislators and citizens who developed the Superfund Act had hoped the program would allow EPA to clean up the contaminated areas across the country. However, they greatly underestimated the size of the problem. The overwhelming number of sites, the huge costs, and poor leadership early in the program prevented Superfund from making significant progress.

The total number of sites removed from the NPL by July 1991 was only 34. Each one required more than five years of work from start to finish. Several billion dollars has already been spent. In one study alone, about $800,000 went to determine what chemicals were escaping from a site. Some experts predict that more than $100 billion will eventually be needed to clean up the remaining sites.

In addition to the high number of problem sites and cleanup costs, other difficulties got the Superfund off to a troubled start.

The first managers of the Superfund program helped contribute to its problems. A few of the early decisions by leading EPA officials delayed important actions by the agency. After an investigation of the EPA, several leaders resigned or were fired. One former EPA official even went to jail for perjury—lying under oath.

Some of the actions taken by the EPA at cleanup sites have also come under fire. Critics say the actions were short-term solutions, and, in some cases, just moved the pollution from one place to another.

Another problem with Superfund is that the money from the program cannot be used to compensate individuals affected by the wastes. Many people feel that the fund should also help the victims of the disasters.

In 1986, President Ronald Reagan signed into law a major revision of the original Superfund Act, called the Superfund Amendments and Reauthorization Act. An important feature was increased financial support of $8.5 billion for the program.

Technicians looking like aliens from outer space collect and study some of the hazardous waste that has accumulated at a Superfund site.

The Right to Know

One of the major problems following the disaster in Bhopal, India, was the lack of any organized system to alert nearby residents of the emergency and to treat victims. It clearly showed the need for disaster plans prepared in advance of emergencies.

In the United States, the Emergency Planning and Community Right-to-Know Act was signed into law. The law recognizes that accidents will happen but that their impact can be reduced with proper planning.

A part of this law, the Emergency Planning section, is designed to help communities prepare to handle hazardous-waste disasters. A committee is formed in each community to develop plans for emergency action, and to teach proper and quick methods of response to chemical emergencies.

The Community Right-to-Know section of the law requires industries to report all hazardous substances they use and the amount they release into the environment.

This new information provides the public and local governments with a complete inventory of the chemicals being released into their local air and water. The information is used to develop new regulations and standards to control these chemicals. Contact your local Emergency Planning Committee to find out about your community's plan.

Leaking Underground Storage Tanks

Sometime when you're at a gas station, you may see an employee drop a long pole through an opening in the ground. He's doing this to measure the amount of gasoline in an underground storage tank. The measurement that he gets will be compared to the last measurement taken and the

Steel tanks buried underground gradually corrode, leaking their contents into the soil. Both the tank and the contaminated soil must be handled as hazardous waste.

amount of gasoline sold, to determine if any gas is leaking from the tank.

This is a common method of measuring, but it would take weeks, maybe even years, to discover small leaks this way. So, drop by drop, gasoline can enter the ground.

A leak amounting to only a water glass full of gasoline can contaminate more than 1 million gallons (3.8 million liters) of groundwater, which is enough to keep 36 people supplied with water for one year.

FACT

There are more than three million underground storage tanks, according to EPA estimates, and thousands of these tanks are leaking. Many more are expected to begin leaking as the rusting process continues to take its toll. Serious health problems may be the result. Groundwater contaminated with gasoline can cause headaches and other illnesses, even cancer.

Thanks to an amendment to RCRA that was passed in 1986, the EPA and individual states have the authority to take action on leaking underground storage tanks (LUST).

A small tax on gasoline funds the program, which requires carefully monitoring of more than one million tanks. Damaged tanks must be replaced with new tanks that include leak detection systems.

The various laws and regulations have changed how hazardous wastes are handled in the United States. Before the passage of the new regulations, many chemicals were unsafely disposed of. Actually, "disposed of" is not really the correct term. In many cases, the waste has only been moved from one location to another.

Many people are demanding even stronger laws to control hazardous substances—rules that would require industry to prove a product is safe rather than the government having to prove it is harmful.

But just because there are regulations, even tough ones, does not mean that everyone follows them. Greater enforcement is required to stop midnight dumping.

The Strike Force

The increasing number of illegal dumping incidents and the high cost of cleanup have led several communities to form investigation teams.

One of the first investigation teams was formed in Los Angeles, California. The Los Angeles Environmental Crimes

This underground storage tank was used for the illegal storage of hazardous waste, which leaked out into the soil around it.

Strike Force is made up of investigators from the police, fire, sanitation, and health departments. This special environmental team has caught many illegal dumpers and exporters of hazardous wastes.

After receiving reports that a company was collecting hazardous wastes for disposal and dumping them into a sewer, the strike force was called in. The company had been making huge profits by using this disposal method. The investigators closed the plant, examined records, and inspected the facility. The owner was convicted, fined $100,000, and sentenced to three months in jail.

In another case, undercover investigators followed a truck driver who was transporting hazardous wastes across the border into Mexico. The driver loaded drums into his truck, covered them with cardboard and wood, and then hauled them to Mexico. There the driver disposed of the barrels in old factory warehouses. The barrels were filled with various chemicals, solvents, and toxic substances. Strike force members arrested the driver and the waste dealer that made the deal. The two were charged with conspiracy, illegal disposal, and the export of hazardous wastes. Both people could face more than 25 years in jail.

The message to company owners is clear. If a company knowingly dumps hazardous wastes illegally and is caught, the owner will be fined and possibly put in jail.

On the national level, the EPA has trained enforcement agents. They have the same authority to enforce toxic substance laws that the federal marshals have. However, the 32 agents have a great number of cases to handle all around the country. The strike force will need to be expanded before most waste dealers will worry.

A better solution lies in getting companies to govern their own methods of dealing with chemicals.

In the wake of the *Exxon Valdez* oil spill, which dumped millions of gallons of oil into the water off the Alaskan coast in 1989, environmentalists decided it was time for industries to follow ethical guidelines that would protect the environment.

A group of investors, investment professionals, and environmental organizations formed the Coalition for Envi-

THE VALDEZ PRINCIPLES

By adopting these principles, we publicly affirm our belief that corporations and their shareholders have a direct responsibility for the environment. We believe that corporations must conduct their business as responsible stewards of the environment, and seek profits only in a manner that leaves the Earth healthy and safe. We believe that corporations must not compromise the ability of future generations to sustain their needs.

We recognize this to be a long-term commitment to update our practices continually in light of advances in technology and new understandings in health and environmental science. We intend to make consistent, measurable progress in implementing these principles and to apply them wherever we operate throughout the world.

1. **PROTECTION OF THE BIOSPHERE**

We will minimize and strive to eliminate the release of any pollutant that may cause environmental damage to the air, water, or Earth or its inhabitants. We will safeguard habitats in rivers, lakes, wetlands, coastal zones, and oceans and will minimize contributing to the greenhouse effect, depletion of the ozone layer, acid rain, or smog.

2. **SUSTAINABLE USE OF NATURAL RESOURCES**

We will make sustainable use of natural resources, such as water, soils, and forests. We will conserve nonrenewable natural resources through efficient use and careful planning. We will protect wildlife habitat, open spaces, and wilderness, while preserving biodiversity.

3. **REDUCTION AND DISPOSAL OF WASTE**

We will minimize the creation of waste, especially hazardous waste, and wherever possible recycle materials. We will dispose of all wastes through safe and responsible methods.

4. **WISE USE OF ENERGY**

We will make every effort to use environmentally safe and sustainable energy sources to meet our needs. We will invest in improved energy efficiency and conservation in our operations. We will maximize the energy efficiency of products we produce or sell.

ronmentally Responsible Economics. They wrote a list of guidelines that they hope investors will use to evaluate corporations, and that corporations will adopt as their own. These guidelines are called the Valdez Principles. K-Mart and Chrysler are two companies that have adopted these principles. Many of the principles can help guide our own lives, too, as each of us makes an effort to preserve the environment by reducing our use of hazardous substances.

5. RISK REDUCTION

We will minimize the environmental, health, and safety risks to our employees and the communities in which we operate by employing safe technologies and operating procedures and by being constantly prepared for emergencies.

6. MARKETING OF SAFE PRODUCTS AND SERVICES

We will sell products or services that minimize adverse environmental impacts and that are safe as consumers commonly use them. We will inform consumers of the environmental impacts of our products or services.

7. DAMAGE COMPENSATION

We will take responsibility for any harm we cause to the environment by making every effort to fully restore the environment and to compensate those persons who are adversely affected.

8. DISCLOSURE

We will disclose to our employees and to the public incidents relating to our operations that cause environmental harm or pose health or safety hazards. We will disclose potential environmental, health or safety hazards posed by our operations, and we will not take any action against employees who report any condition that creates a danger to the environment or poses health and safety hazards.

9. ENVIRONMENTAL DIRECTORS AND MANAGERS

At least one member of the board of directors will be a person qualified to represent environmental interests. We will commit management resources to implement these principles, including the funding of an office of vice president for environmental affairs or an equivalent executive position, reporting directly to the CEO, to monitor and report upon our implementation efforts.

10. ASSESSMENT AND ANNUAL AUDIT

We will conduct and make public an annual self-evaluation of our progress in implementing these principles and in complying with all applicable laws and regulations throughout our worldwide operations. We will work toward the timely creation of independent environmental audit procedures, which we will complete annually and make available to the public.

Chapter 8

Pollution Prevention:
The Only Solution

OUR PAST EXPERIENCES have shown us that there is no such place as "away" where we can throw things.

Our land, water, and air are not dumping grounds, yet they're used for disposing of millions of tons of hazardous wastes each year. Although such waste-treatment methods as incineration, neutralization, and biological reduction decrease the danger, they do not solve the problem. The only solution to the problems posed by hazardous waste and toxic substances is to reduce or eliminate their production.

The idea of reducing pollution at the source rather than trying to clean it up afterward is still relatively new. The EPA recently recommended the following ways to handle hazardous waste, in order of importance:

1. First, prevent all the pollution possible by reducing or eliminating the production of hazardous wastes.

2. Utilize waste-exchange programs for materials that can have secondary uses.

3. Recycle waste materials.

4. Provide waste-treatment methods to reduce the volume of the remaining hazardous waste.

5. And only as a last resort, when no other methods can be used, should hazardous waste be disposed of in "secured" landfills.

The choice is clear. The only long-term solution to hazardous waste is to stop producing it. One easy way to accomplish this would be to stop production of things like cars, various metals, paints, televisions, toys, synthetic clothing, fertilizers, and thousands of other products. Of course, this isn't really practical. However, something can be done to eliminate production of hazardous waste.

The first step in a company's pollution prevention program is to complete a *waste minimization audit*. This is a full investigation into how a company uses, stores, transports, and disposes of hazardous materials. From this investigation a list of potential changes is developed and evaluated. Then, methods are suggested that the company can use to reduce or eliminate hazardous wastes. The emphasis is on waste *reduction*, not waste *disposal*.

Ways to Reduce Waste

One of the best and easiest methods of reducing wastes is by improving operations. Employees who handle hazardous substances should be carefully trained to take more care in the way they transport and handle chemicals. This helps eliminate spills and accidents. Employees that are well trained will also be better able to respond to accidents, reducing the threat of injury to themselves and the environment.

Equipment can be changed to make the manufacturing process more efficient—producing less waste without affecting the quality of the product. A strict maintenance program for equipment should prevent leaks and keep equipment operating efficiently.

Many companies around the world are experimenting with ways to reduce hazardous wastes. They're trying new manufacturing processes, new formulas, and new chemicals. The rising costs of disposal and treatment, the increasing rules and regulations, and public protests have encouraged companies to test these changes. The efforts of many companies have been encouraging.

In Milwaukee, Wisconsin, a printing company invested

Chemicals used to dry-clean clothing can be collected, recycled, and reused.

in a bold, expensive change. Faced with putting in expensive pollution-control equipment to reduce its hazardous waste, the company changed its printing process, going from solvent-based ink to water-based ink.

After adding expensive new equipment and experiencing many headaches trying to complete the transition, the company was successful. They reduced their wastes, while still managing to provide a high-quality product. And they will recover the costs they invested in less than five years.

In another example, the Department of Defense estimates that it used to take about 340 hours to strip the paint off an F-4 fighter plane. Using this old process, more than 10,000 pounds (4,500 kilograms) of a wet-paint sludge were produced. But the department is now using a new method, called plastics media blasting. Small plastic beads are sprayed on the plane's surface, hitting the paint and removing it by abrasion. The beads can be used again, and hazardous substances are no longer produced. Waste was reduced to 320 pounds (144 kilograms) and the job takes only 40 hours to complete—a tremendous savings.

Other companies have changed painting methods. An electric company changed to a water-based paint from an

Pollution control equipment at 3M's videotape plant in Hutchinson, Minnesota, still under construction early in 1990. The system removes solvent vapors from exhaust air and purifies them for reuse in manufacturing.

oil-based paint, resulting in a 97 percent decrease in the amount of paint sludge, a hazardous waste. An automobile maker modified its painting process—it's now fully enclosed, so excess paint can be captured and recycled.

The 3M Company, in 1975, started the "3P" program, which stands for "Pollution Prevention Pays." The program's goal was to reduce or eliminate pollutants at the source, thereby saving cleanup or disposal costs. All employees at 3M plants around the world participate.

In a 3M plant that produces fire-fighting products, two hazardous chemicals were eliminated. Not only were the replacement chemicals non-hazardous, but they were less expensive as well. In another move, 3M changed its method of handling aluminum sulfate, a hazardous waste produced as a by-product of making videotapes. The company used to dispose of it, but now, through a waste-exchange program, they sell the material to fertilizer plants. These plants convert the aluminum sulfate into plant food.

During the last ten years, 3M has reduced wastes by more than 40 percent, thanks to new production systems and the use of non-hazardous substitutes in place of harmful chemicals. Company officials estimate that the changes have saved 3M over $350 million.

In 1989, the company announced that it was stepping up its efforts with the introduction of a new program, "3P Plus." This program should reduce all hazardous and non-hazardous emissions by 90 percent, and will cut the generation of hazardous wastes in half by the year 2000. Pollution prevention *does* pay.

Benefits

In an EPA study on waste reduction, more than 40 percent of the firms that deliberately reduced their waste recovered all of the money they invested in just one year.

There are many broad, long-term benefits to waste reduction programs, such as:

- fewer accidents and spills during handling;
- less employee exposure to hazardous substances;
- less hazardous waste as the by-product of the production of chemicals;
- reduced future Superfund sites for the next generation;
- reduced long-term liability of companies to clean up waste sites; and
- less household hazardous wastes mixed with garbage.

Incentives

Waste-reduction techniques have proven successful. It's time for all companies and agencies to develop such techniques. Other countries around the world are investing money in waste-reduction research. Denmark and the Netherlands have each invested more than $7 million per year to clean up manufacturing processes. No country has totally eliminated the production of hazardous waste, so research continues.

The United States needs to increase its efforts. In 1988, the EPA budgeted less than $1 million to support waste reduction. The agency needs to increase the reasons for industries to research and install waste-reduction systems. With support from government, industries, and citizens, waste-reduction programs will increase the safety of the world we live in.

A recovery service collecting used automobile fluids at a service station. Many such fluids could be recovered and recycled rather than thrown away.

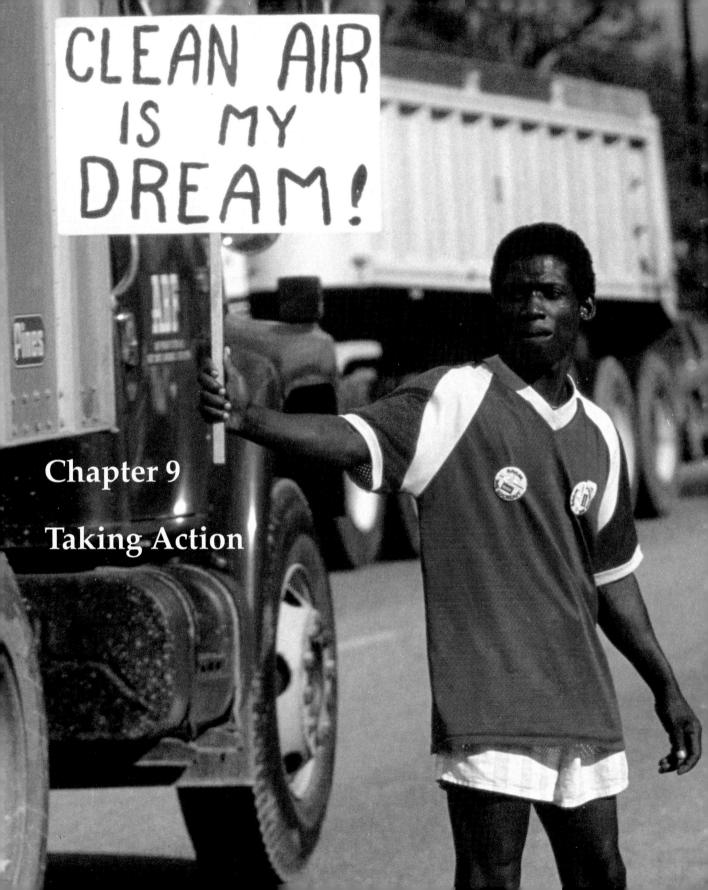

CLEAN AIR
IS MY
DREAM!

Chapter 9

Taking Action

 AN OLD CHINESE PROVERB states: "Unless we change direction, we are likely to end up where we are headed." It seems a particularly fitting saying to describe our problems with hazardous substances.

The issues surrounding hazardous wastes are relatively new. PCBs have been used for only 50 years, dioxins are even younger. We're using thousands of chemicals today that may cause dangerous situations tomorrow—but we just don't know. Our society has placed an emphasis on short-term gain, not long-term responsibility. We are still following that direction today and we are likely to get where we are headed.

The direction that we need to go in order to protect our planet requires that we change. The new direction needs to take into consideration more than just short-term cleanup, safe waste disposal, and waste destruction. With populations growing, new chemicals being developed, and everyone wanting a higher standard of living, we need to consider long-term consequences. The solution is reduction of waste. We need to "Think Globally and Act Locally."

We as individuals must take action. In the story *The Lorax* by Dr. Seuss, there is a one-word message near the end of the story. It is "UNLESS." The meaning of the word becomes perfectly clear when Dr. Seuss writes at the conclusion, "UNLESS someone like you cares a whole awful lot, nothing is going to get better. It's not."

You are the person that must care. Each of us must take responsibility for our impact on the environment. As individuals we have many opportunities to help change the way our society handles hazardous wastes.

These photos from the Household Hazardous Waste Project show us a selection of common household cleaning products that contain harmful chemicals (left) *and some safer alternatives* (right).

Taking Personal Action

There are many things you and your family can do to reduce the dangers of hazardous substances:

1. Avoid using harmful products whenever you can. Review the recommended alternatives listed in Chapter 4 to reduce hazardous wastes in your home.

2. Keep informed. Determine what hazardous wastes are being generated in your community and learn how they are disposed of.

3. Find out whether your community has complied with the Federal Community Right-To-Know Law.

4. Start an environmental organization at school to sponsor cleanup events, public information efforts, and guest environmental speakers. The organization could encourage the school district to expand environmental education in the curriculum.

5. Work with your neighbors to organize a community Clean Sweep.

6. Organize a community meeting to discuss hazardous substances. Invite local companies and encourage them to conduct a hazardous-substances audit to determine the waste-reduction techniques they can use.

7. Use fewer pesticides in your yard. Instead, develop a pest-management program that uses natural predators, dis-

ease-resistant plants, and natural substitutes for pesticides.

8. Use rechargeable household batteries instead of throw-away batteries. Americans throw away more than 2.5 billion batteries each year. They come from watches, radios, cameras, calculators, remote-controlled toys, etc. These batteries contain hazardous chemicals, such as mercury, lead, nickel, and cadmium.

9. Assist others in your community in establishing a battery-recycling center for disposable batteries. These facilities are common in Europe.

10. Do not use room deodorizers that contain paradichlorobenzene (PDCB).

11. For your safety, wear the proper safety equipment recommended on product labels.

12. Continue to learn about hazardous-waste issues.

Shop Wisely

1. Carefully read labels and take responsibility for proper use and disposal of hazardous substances.

2. Ask your local grocery and hardware stores to carry non-toxic alternatives to hazardous household products.

3. Buy the least-hazardous products available. Items marked **DANGER** are the most toxic. Products marked **WARNING** are moderately toxic. And **CAUTION** means less toxic.

4. Use latex-based paints. They are water-based paints that do not require solvents to clean them up.

5. Reduce, reuse, and recycle as many products as you can. This conserves resources, saves energy, and reduces the quantity of hazardous waste generated when making the product.

6. Avoid excessive packaging to assist in reducing the amount of plastic and paper purchased.

7. Buy unbleached paper products such as coffee filters, toilet paper, and paper towels. In the process to produce "white" paper products, large amounts of chlorine are used, creating a hazardous waste. Some countries have banned the sale of chlorine-bleached products.

Neighbors can help limit hazardous wastes by exchanging leftover paint and other products.

Express Your Opinion

Contact your elected officials to see where they stand on current hazardous-waste issues. Also examine their past voting record on these issues. Then encourage your parents and other adults to vote for people who have a good record on the issue and are willing to work to improve the situation.

Let your public officials, both elected and appointed, know exactly what you think. Recommend that they initiate action at their level to:

1. Support further research to provide technologies that will reduce or eliminate hazardous wastes.

2. Pass laws that require accurate and uniform labeling on products so people know exactly what they are buying. This should encourage consumers to buy alternative products and discourage companies from using hazardous wastes.

3. Develop international laws to control the exportation of hazardous wastes to foreign countries.

4. Prohibit the sale of hazardous products banned in the United States to foreign countries.

5. Increase financial support for Superfund projects.

6. Provide incentives for companies to begin hazardous-waste reduction programs.

7. Require increased study and research on new chemicals being introduced by companies.

You can also share your opinion on issues by writing an editorial for your school newspaper or community paper, or by participating in a radio call-in program.

Writing Letters. In writing a letter in which you express your opinion on controversial issues, follow these seven tips:

1. Make your letter one page or less. Cover only one subject in each letter.

2. Introduce yourself and tell why you, personally, are for or against the issue.

3. Be clear and to the point.

4. Be specific on whether you want the person to vote "yes" or "no."

5. Write as an individual. The environmental groups you belong to will have already let the legislator know their stand on the issue.

6. When you get a response, write a follow-up letter to re-emphasize your position and give your reaction to your legislator's comments.

7. Write again to thank your legislators if they vote the way you asked them to.

On issues concerning state legislation or to express your opinion about actions taken by your state or provincial environmental or natural resources agency, you can write to:

Your local state or provincial legislator. Check at your local library to discover his or her name.

The governor of your state or premier of your province. Write in care of your state or provincial capital.

The director of your state or province's department of natural resources or related environmental agency. Check your local library for the specific person and the address.

On issues concerning federal legislation or to express your opinion about actions taken by the federal government, you can write to:

Your two state senators. Check at your local library to discover their names.

> The Honorable _____
> U.S. Senate
> Washington, DC 20510

Your local congressman. Check at your local library to discover his or her name.

> The Honorable _____
> U.S. House of Representatives
> Washington, DC 20515

Your local provincial or federal member of Parliament. Check at your local library to discovery his or her name.

> The Honorable _____
> House of Commons
> Ottawa, Ontario, Canada K1A 0A6

The President of the United States. He has the power to veto, or turn down, bills approved by the Senate and the House of Representatives as well as to introduce bills of his own. He also has final control over what the U.S. Environmental Protection Agency and other agencies do.

> President _____
> The White House
> 1600 Pennsylvania Avenue, NW
> Washington, DC 20501
>
> *The Prime Minister of Canada.*
> The Honorable _____
> House of Commons
> Ottawa, Ontario, Canada K1A 0A6

Join Organizations

Join environmental organizations that are concerned with hazardous-waste issues. Investigate to see if you can join any local chapters that are taking action on projects in your community. By joining, you are saying that you support their work on behalf of the environment. Contact the following:

Citizens for a Better Environment, 111 King Street, Madison, WI 53703

Citizens Clearinghouse for Hazardous Wastes, Inc., P.O.Box 6806, Falls Church, VA 22040

Clean Water Project, 317 Pennsylvania Ave., SE, Washington, DC 20003

Environmental Action Foundation, 1525 New Hampshire Ave., NW, Washington, DC 20036

Lake Michigan Federation, 647 W. Virginia St., Milwaukee, WI 53204

League of Women Voters, 1730 M St., NW, Washington, DC 20036

National Audubon Society, 950 3rd St., New York, NY 10022

National Toxics Campaign, 37 Temple Place, 4th Floor, Boston, MA 02111

National Wildlife Federation, 1400 16th St., NW, Washington, DC 20036

Sierra Club, 730 Polk St., San Francisco, CA 94109

World Resources Institute, 1709 New York Ave., NW, Washington, DC 20006

Worldwatch Institute, 1776 Massachusetts Ave., Washington, DC 20036

Unless. . .

Many of these actions are simple and require little or no sacrifice. They're just a matter of changing some habits. These actions will make your community a better and safer place to live. Remember: "UNLESS" you care, nothing will get better.

This commercial hazardous-waste landfill in South Carolina is only 600 feet (180 meters) from a lake that is part of the largest water system in the state. It lies directly above three aquifers that supply fresh water to residents of the area. There is no such thing as a landfill that is totally safe. The only answer is for companies and individuals to eliminate as much hazardous waste as possible.

GLOSSARY

acute – quick, sudden; refers to a short exposure to a hazardous substance.

aquifer – a body of underground water, usually in porous rocks, that may provide water for wells.

bioaccumulation – a process in which pesticides or heavy metals can build up more and more in each level of the food chain.

birth defects – disorders found in babies, either inherited or caused by chemicals.

by-product – something that is produced during the manufacture of another product.

cancer – a harmful, uncontrolled growth of cells in the body that can destroy healthy tissue and organs.

carcinogen – any substance that causes cancer.

chain reaction – a series of actions in which one sets off another, especially referring to nuclear fission, to produce power.

chronic – long-lasting and of low intensity; refers to exposure to a hazardous substance.

contamination – an impurity.

core – the area in a nuclear reactor that contains the fuel.

corrosive – having the ability to eat away a substance by chemical action, such as certain types of hazardous wastes.

detoxification – the process of making toxic substances harmless by treating them in a variety of methods.

dioxin – a very complex chemical that is a toxic by-product in the production of various herbicides.

EPA – see **United States Environmental Protection Agency**

epidemiology – the study of diseases that affect large numbers of people.

flammable – burnable; having the ability to ignite easily.

food chain – the flow of nutrients and energy through a series of living organisms. The first link, producer, is eaten by a consumer, which in turn is eaten by a second-level consumer. Example: algae→smelt→heron.

groundwater – water found below the Earth's surface.

hazardous – capable of harming the environment or causing illness or death to living things.

herbicide – a substance used to kill various plants.

incineration – the process of burning waste materials.

infectious – contagious, able to be spread by contact.

insecticide – a substance used to kill specific insects.

landfill – a place where solid wastes are buried. A *secured* landfill is one constructed to hold hazardous solid wastes.

leachate – water contaminated by contact with hazardous substances, which escapes from a landfill into the groundwater.

meltdown – an accidental heating of the core of a nuclear reactor so that it melts into the ground.

midnight dumping – illegal dumping of hazardous wastes.

monitor – to measure the level of pollution, usually in air or water, by taking samples.

mutation – a change in the genetic material that determines characteristics of offspring. It can be caused by a number of chemicals or radiation.

pesticide – a substance that is used to kill harmful plants and animals.

pollutant – any material that is harmful to living organisms.

ppm – parts per million, a measure of the concentration of a substance in air or water.

radioactive waste – any waste material that contains radioactivity, usually from a nuclear reactor, medical tests, or nuclear weapons production.

reactor – the device in which a controlled nuclear reaction takes place to produce electric power.

sediment – any material, previously suspended in water, that settles onto a surface.

synthetic – made by people, as opposed to occurring naturally.

toxic – in general, harmful to people and other organisms; more specifically, poisonous.

United States Environmental Protection Agency (EPA) – a government agency established in 1970 to review, approve, and monitor programs and projects related to the environment.

INDEX

Bold number = Illustration

PHOTO SOURCES

AP/Wide World Photos: 92

Batelle Pacific Northwest Laboratories: 85

The Bettman Archive: 15, 17, 18, 19

Photo by Marsha Boone, courtesy of H.H.W.P.: 116 (both), 118

Chemical Manufacturers Association: 31

Chemical Waste Management, Inc.: 79, 82, 83, 87 (top left), 88 (both), 89

Citizens Asking for a Safe Environment: 122

Barbara Kelly: 48, 55

Sam Kittner, Photographer: 42, 114

Laidlaw Environmental Services Inc.: 52, 57, 67, 74

Lake Michigan Federation: 26, 40 (top right),

K. Martensen/Greenpeace: 44

Photo Courtesy of Ministry of the Environment, Ontario, Canada: 77

New York State Department of Environmental Conservation: 6, 9, 11, 13 (both)

NOAA: Hazardous Materials Response Branch: 29, 33, 37, 47, 87(top right), 96, 100, 104

David Noton/Firth Photo:14

Ontario Waste Management Corporation: 32

Pickaver/Greenpeace: 40 (top left)

Public Health Service/U.S. Department of Health and Human Services: 36

Safety-Kleen Corporation: 111, 113

Al Stenstrup/Havenwoods Environmental Awareness Center: 49, 94

Tass/Sovfoto: 23

Courtesy of 3M: 112

Times Beach EPA Information Center: 21

United States Army Photographs: 76

United States Department of Energy: 62, 71 (both)

United States Department of Transportation: 12, 16, 33, 70, 77, 90

Photo courtesy of Union Carbide: 68, 69

Roy F. Weston, Inc.: 38 (bottom), 39, 101

Ryan Williams/Firth Photo: 2

R. Winslow/Greenpeace: 28

Wisconsin Department of Natural Resources: 38 (top), 43, 54, 60, 63, 65, 103, 108

ABOUT THE AUTHOR

Allen Stenstrup is a former middle school science teacher. After completing his masters degree at Northern Illinois University, he directed the development of the Havenwoods Environmental Awareness Center in Milwaukee. He is currently working on Remedial Action Plans for the Sheboygan River and the Milwaukee Estuary for the Wisconsin Department of Natural Resources. Al conducts teacher workshops on a variety of environmental issues and teaches both education and environmental courses at the University of Wisconsin-Milwaukee. Al and his wife, Geri, live with their two sons, Corey and B.J., in Germantown, Wisconsin.